THE EVERYTHING

PARENT'S GUIDE TO

SPECIAL EDUCATION

Dear Reader,

During the years I taught in a regular education classroom, I was always particularly drawn to my students who had trouble learning or adhering to the classroom routine. There was something more vulnerable about those children, and I had to work a little harder to teach them.

Eventually, I left the classroom to work in early childhood special education, working with evaluators, parents, and service providers to help children with disabilities get the services they needed to keep up with their nondisabled peers. I thought I had a sense of how hard it is for parents to advocate for their children in a system they don't understand, but it wasn't until I was on the other side of the table that I truly understood how overwhelming the special education process could be.

As a parent of a child with a disability, I found myself in the midst of a contentious battle to find my child eligible for special education services and provide him with a free appropriate public education (FAPE). I was successful, mostly due to my knowledge of the process and the law. But I started wondering: What happens to parents who don't know their child's rights or how the special education system works?

Since then, I've spent a lot of time advising parents so they know how to advocate for their child. In writing this book, I hope to do this on a larger scale. Good luck and remember—you are your child's best advocate!

Amanda Morin

WELCOME TO THE

EVERYTHING®
PARENT'S GUIDES

Everything® Parent's Guides are a part of the bestselling Everything® series and cover common parenting issues like childhood illnesses and tantrums, as well as medical conditions like asthma and juvenile diabetes. These family-friendly books are designed to be a one-stop guide for parents. If you want authoritative information on specific topics not fully covered in other books, Everything® Parent's Guides are your perfect solution.

QUESTION

Answers to
common questions

FACT

Important snippets
of information

ALERT

Urgent
warnings

ESSENTIAL

Quick
handy tips

When you're done reading, you can finally say you know **EVERYTHING®**!

PUBLISHER Karen Cooper

MANAGING EDITOR, EVERYTHING® SERIES Lisa Laing

COPY CHIEF Casey Ebert

ASSISTANT PRODUCTION EDITOR Alex Guarco

ACQUISITIONS EDITOR Pamela Wissman

DEVELOPMENT EDITOR Brett Palana-Shanahan

EVERYTHING® SERIES COVER DESIGNER Erin Alexander

Visit the entire Everything® series at *www.everything.com*

THE
EVERYTHING®

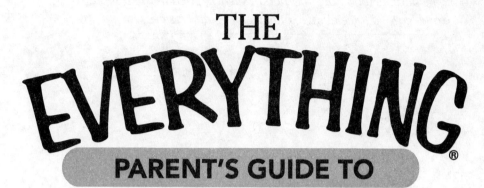

PARENT'S GUIDE TO

SPECIAL
EDUCATION

A complete step-by-step guide to advocating
for your child with special needs

Amanda Morin

adamsmedia

Avon, Massachusetts

To all the parents who have worried in silence, cried in frustration,
and learned to celebrate small victories and successes.

An Everything® Series Book.
Everything® and everything.com® are registered trademarks of F+W Media, Inc.

Published by
Adams Media, a division of F+W Media, Inc.
57 Littlefield Street, Avon, MA 02322. U.S.A.
www.adamsmedia.com

ISBN 10: 1-4405-6967-3
ISBN 13: 978-1-4405-6967-8
eISBN 10: 1-4405-6968-1
eISBN 13: 978-1-4405-6968-5

Printed in the United States of America.

10 9 8 7 6 5 4 3 2 1

This book is available at quantity discounts for bulk purchases.
For information, please call 1-800-289-0963.

Contents

Acknowledgments

This book was a labor of love and I owe a debt of gratitude to so many people who helped along the way. Thank you to the countless parents with whom I have talked for sharing your stories and trusting me enough to ask for help navigating the system. A special thank you to Joselyn, Margaret, Charlie, Esther, and Jennifer K. who all told me I *had* to write this book sooner rather than later.

I'm grateful to my editor, Pamela Wissman, who, among other things, tirelessly answered many e-mails that began, "This may be a weird question, but . . . " I also owe thanks to development editor, Brett Palana-Shanahan and the rest of the incredible team at Adams Media.

Thank you also to Dr. Andrew Kahn, who walked me through his evaluation process and various assessment tools, and for being an incredible advocate for the children he works with.

Thank you to my son Jacob for opening my eyes to the fact that the parent experience with special education is very different than the professional experience, and to my other children, Megan and Benjamin, for being patient and understanding when I wasn't always available. Lastly, I am always thankful for the support of my husband, Jon, who understands that "five more minutes" means I might still be writing two hours later.

Spe • cial Ed • u • ca • tion

(ˈspeSHəl ˌejəˈkāSHən)

(n) Services, programs, and instruction specially designed to meet the individual educational needs of a student with a disability

Introduction

IF YOU'RE READING THIS book, you probably have a child who has or may have a disability and you are concerned. Maybe your child is struggling in school and you don't know how to get help. Perhaps your child has been referred for Response to Intervention or for further evaluation for special education services, and you're not really sure what all of that means. Or maybe your child is already receiving special education services, and you're not happy with how it's working and you don't know what to do about it.

Whatever the circumstances, you picked up this book because you wanted to know more about the special education process and how to navigate it to make sure your child gets the right help to make school easier. You are not alone in needing this help. Many parents feel helpless in the face of what seems like a daunting, tangled system of rules and regulations.

Sometimes sitting in meetings to talk about your child's strengths and weaknesses, and what services are available to a child "with that diagnosis," can feel more like a contract negotiation than a conversation about an actual child. It can be frustrating and overwhelming to balance being your child's advocate with the need to work cooperatively with the school district to help your child.

This comprehensive, easy-to-read book is designed to teach you what you need to know about the laws that govern special education, the process of referring your child for special education, and what will happen once your child is referred. It's designed to answer the question "What's next?" before you even have to ask it. It will walk you through the process of keeping organized records, asking the right questions, finding the right answers, and even what to do if you and the school district can't come to an agreement on what type of program your child should have.

No two children who need special education services are the same, but they are all covered by the same legal rights provided to them by the groundbreaking Individuals with Disabilities Education Act (IDEA). IDEA has changed the landscape of special education and gives parents like you the power of an equal say in deciding what your child's educational program looks like.

Throughout this book, special education programs are referred to as "special education services" or "special education." Non–special education programs are "regular education" or the "general education" classroom. That doesn't mean that your child is irregular; it's simply a way to differentiate between the types of programs.

Knowing what these terms (and many others) mean and how they pertain to your child can serve to make you not only a good advocate but an informed one as well. Being able to back up your position with more than just a gut feeling can alleviate a feeling of helplessness and replace it with a feeling of satisfaction and purpose.

You will learn about the wide variety of disabilities children who qualify for special education have and the varied effects these disabilities can have on their ability to learn in the general education classroom. No matter what type of disability your child has, you will learn what types of services are available, what accommodations might be helpful, and how to work with the school to create an individualized education plan to meet your child's needs. Together, we can unravel that tangled system so you are confident enough to have a meeting about *your* child, not a negotiation for what services are given to a child with a certain diagnosis.

CHAPTER 1

The Basics of Special Education

Until 1975, if you asked the question "What is special education?" the answer you got would be incredibly dependent upon whom you asked. One parent of a child with a disability might tell you it meant her child couldn't go to school with the neighborhood children; another parent might tell you that special education was the classroom where kids with physical or mental disabilities were taught away from the "regular" kids. Still others, both teachers and parents, might not even know what you were talking about if you asked them.

What Special Education Is

In 1975, Congress passed Public Law 94-142, the Education for All Handicapped Children Act. The law laid out a set of rules, regulations, and legal protections for children with disabilities that had never been seen before. It has been revised many times and, in 1990, was renamed the Individuals with Disabilities Education Act (IDEA).

According to IDEA, the basic answer to the question about special education is simple: "Special education means specially designed instruction, at no cost to the parents, to meet the unique needs of a child with a disability." (IDEA, Sec. 300, Subsection/paragraph 39)

IDEA's simple answer doesn't mean that special education is simple, though, and it doesn't mean it looks the same for every child. In fact, IDEA makes sure that special education *doesn't* look the same for every child. That's exactly what "specially designed instruction" means; your child's special education program will be created specifically to meet her individual needs.

FACT

While your child's plan is called an IEP (individualized education program), the term is also used to refer to the meeting that is held about your child's special education. It's not unusual to hear that you will be writing an IEP at the IEP.

Although it may sound a little backward, in order to make sure that children with disabilities are able to have that specially designed program, IDEA lays out rules that apply to all children receiving special education services. Those legally binding instructions provide the basics you'll need to know in order to be the best advocate you can be for your child.

An Overview of Special Education Services

You already know that if your child has a disability that affects his education, he's entitled to an educational program that is built around his needs.

However, now you need to know what IDEA says about how to make that happen. Some of the more important points you should know are:

- Your child has the right to a free appropriate public education (FAPE). This means that your child has the legal right to the same education as his peers without disabilities—without you having to pay for it. The school district must, at public expense, provide the support services, individualized instruction, and/or modifications your child needs to be able to learn what other kids are learning.
- Your child has the right to a full evaluation to determine what his needs are and whether or not he has a disability that qualifies him for special education. This evaluation must be performed by the local education agency. (The local education agency is the school district or, for non-school-age children, the agency that provides early intervention services.) This evaluation cannot be done without your consent unless there is a hearing that rules against you.
- Your child has the right to receive his education in an environment most like his nondisabled peers that will still allow him to learn. He's entitled to stay in his neighborhood school if a FAPE can be provided there, or if the school can't provide such a placement, then he has the right to a private school placement at the expense of the local education agency.
- If it is determined that your child has a disability, he has the right to an individualized education program (IEP) with yearly, easily measured educational goals. The IEP is written by and agreed upon by a team that includes involved school personnel, evaluators, service providers, and, most importantly, you.
- Parents have the right to ask for a hearing if they disagree with the local education agency about their child's IEP, program, placement, or eligibility for special education. Furthermore, no changes can be made to an IEP without your permission or agreement.

The bottom line is that special education services look different for every child, but every child has legal rights in regard to how his or her program is developed and put into place. As you navigate the special education system, keep in mind that your child's IEP only addresses the educational needs that are affected by his disability. That may seem as though he's not getting all he needs, but if he can excel with partial support, that's a good thing!

ALERT

Although IDEA gives your child the right to a FAPE and an individualized program, it doesn't say that the school has to provide the ideal or best program possible. The school is only required to provide a reasonable and "appropriate education" based on your child's needs.

Who Receives Special Education Services?

Special education services aren't just available for children between kindergarten and high school. Your child can actually receive special education services between three and twenty-one years of age.

That may seem like a wide age range, but there are practical reasons for it. Once children turn three, they are technically of preschool age. Whether your child is actually in a preschool or not, under the law it's now time to look at how her disability affects her learning. If your child is already receiving early intervention services, your case manager will hold a transition meeting, changing her plan from family-based services to educationally-based services.

If she is not in preschool and her disability would make it difficult for her to learn in the same type of preschool education as her peers, it is likely that the services on the plan will include some sort of educational instruction, be it tutoring or placement in a preschool setting.

ESSENTIAL

Under IDEA, provisions are made for special education services for children ages birth to three. These services are known as *early intervention*. The eligibility, types of services, and how they are delivered is different than school-based special education.

Having an age limit of twenty-one is also done for a valid reason. If your child has a disability so severe that it significantly impairs her learning and daily functioning, acquiring all of the skills necessary to graduate high school by age eighteen might not be a reasonable goal. Allowing students to continue in special education services until the age of twenty-one provides for better transition planning. It also gives your child some extra time to learn the skills she needs to move from a school environment to the community.

What Kind of Kids Get Special Education Services?

There is no specific profile of kids in special education. They don't all look the same, they don't all act the same, and they don't all have the same needs. If there was a profile or a checklist, it might be a lot easier for some children to get special education services! What can be said about children who receive special education services is this:

- Kids in special education come from all different backgrounds. They are from well-to-do families, middle-class families, and low-income families. They are children whose families have lived in a city for generations, and children whose families are migrant workers.
- Kids in special education have differing abilities, strengths and weaknesses, and varied learning styles. Some learn quickly, while some learn more slowly. Some don't have trouble with learning at all, but they might have trouble with underlying issues that affect their behavior and get in the way of learning. Still others have physical disabilities that make it harder to learn the same way as more "typical" kids.
- Kids in special education receive services because they have been found eligible due to the unique learning needs they have from a specific disability.
- Kids in special education all have plans that are tailored to teach to the way they learn best. Ideally, none of these plans are exactly alike.
- Kids in special education are not "dumb." In fact, some children who receive some special education support also qualify for gifted and talented classes in areas in which they do not have learning problems.
- Kids in special education often receive support services in addition to special education. Those support services, known as "related services," help your child get the most out of his special education program so he can continue to make progress toward his learning goals.

Related Services

Related services can be confusing because, for some children, these services are the only type of special education support they need. Keep in mind that when the teachers, administrators, evaluators, and service providers around you talk about "special education," they are referring specifically to the modifications made to the way your child is being taught what he would learn in a regular classroom.

Remember, your child has the right to an individualized special education *program*. If she needs to be taught differently, that's the special education piece. If she needs other services to help her benefit from that special education and meet her goals, those are "related services." Related services help to make that individualized education a program.

The difference is that related services aren't necessarily educational. For example, a child with a learning disability that makes writing difficult may need access to a computer or other type of device to be able to achieve success in a language arts class. That device, also known as assistive technology, is a related service. In another example, a child who has autism may need occupational therapy services to help learn strategies to cope with his sensitivity to sensory stimuli. Without occupational therapy, that child may not be able to benefit from his education, but with the related service he can.

ALERT

Don't assume the school can automatically deny a service not on this list! Since your child's plan should be individualized to meet his needs, if there are related services he needs that are not on this list, IDEA says the IEP team can make the decision to provide them as needed.

Both of these situations are examples of why IDEA requires schools to give your child related services: to make sure your child is able to "achieve satisfactorily" in the mainstream classroom and to give your child the help she needs to gain benefit from her special education. IDEA includes the following services as related services.

- Psychological services and/or counseling
- Social work services

- Occupational and physical therapy services
- Speech-language and audiology services
- Orientation and mobility services
- Special transportation
- Interpreter services
- Assistive technology
- Medical services (but only for evaluation, not continued care in a school)
- School nurse services

Why Special Education Is Needed

Despite the flexible definition of special education and the frustrations that parents can bump up against when trying to get services for kids, special education is crucial. Without special education services, children who need some support in school or a more structured learning environment would fall behind.

According to a long-term study of students with disabilities done by the U.S. Department of Education's Office of Special Education Programs, kids who don't have adequate special education services to help them are at higher risk for dropping out of school, not just falling behind.

Special education as defined by IDEA allows children to stay in the same school as their neighborhood friends. It provides options for children who, prior to the mid-1970s, were, according to an article in a 1996 edition of the journal *The Future of Children*, routinely denied the right to enroll in school because school administrators considered them to be "uneducable." There has been a lot of progress made in special education since IDEA, and even more progress with its reauthorization in 2004, but that doesn't mean that parents don't have issues with the special education system.

The Parents' View of Special Education

If you're thinking, "All of this is great information, but my child is still struggling in the classroom and we haven't been able to get him the help he needs," you are in good company. Researchers putting together a 2002

Public Agenda report, entitled *When It's Your Own Child: A Report on Special Education from the Families Who Use It*, did a survey of over 500 parents of children with disabilities. The point of the survey was to see what parents' attitudes toward special education was, since for a long time there seemed to be a stigma attached to having your child in special education. It seems now that stigma has lessened and parents are more concerned about how to get those services into place.

It's interesting to note that in the decade since the Public Agenda report was released, there's been a big shift in how many children receive special education services and for what disabilities. While the National Center for Education Statistics reports that the number of students in special education has stayed fairly steady, there has been a 175 percent increase in the system of children with autism, for example.

Here's why that's interesting and how it might apply to your child: If the overall number of kids in special education is staying the same while the number of children with certain disabilities in special education is increasing, that means that it's possible that not all kids who need services are getting them. What parents had to say in the Public Agenda report supported that thought. Some of the highlights of the report are:

- Over half of the parents surveyed said their school district did things the right way when evaluating their children for services, but nearly a third of parents said their child's school was "dragging its feet" in getting the process started.
- A majority of parents (70 percent) said kids "lose out" on getting services because the parents don't know what services are available. Half of the surveyed parents agreed that it's up to parents to figure it out on their own because "the school is not going to volunteer the information."

One parent even went so far as to tell the story of her interaction with a school evaluator who told her if she were less persistent, her child wouldn't be getting services. The moral of this story: You need to know what's available for your child and you need to be persistent.

CHAPTER 2

Special Education Terms Translated

As you start navigating the special education system, there are so many abbreviations, acronyms, and specialized terms that you may feel as though you're wading around in a bowl of alphabet soup. Don't let that discourage you, though, as you may find many of the professionals around the table aren't always sure what everything stands for, either.

What All Those Letters Mean

Although you can always ask for clarification as you need it, here is a brief list of some of the more common terms and acronyms to get you started.

▼ **COMMON SPECIAL EDUCATION ACRONYMS**

Acronym	Stands for
ABA	applied behavior analysis
ABC	antecedent, behavior, consequence
ADA	Americans with Disabilities Act
ADHD	attention deficit hyperactivity disorder
APE	adaptive physical education
AT	assistive technology
AYP	annual yearly progress
BIP	behavioral intervention plan
COTA	certified occupational therapy assistant
DD	developmental disability
DPH	due process hearing
DPHO	due process hearing officer
DSM	*Diagnostic and Statistical Manual of Mental Disorders*
ED	emotional disturbance
EI	early intervention
ESY	extended school year (services)
FAPE	free appropriate public education
FBA	functional behavioral assessment
FERPA	Family Education Rights and Privacy Act
HQT	highly qualified teacher
IDEA	Individuals with Disabilities Education Act
IEE	independent educational evaluation
IEP	individual education program
IFSP	individual family service plan
LD	learning disability
LRE	least restrictive environment
NCLB	No Child Left Behind Act
OCR	Office for Civil Rights
OT	occupational therapy/therapist
PLAAFP	present level of academic achievement and functional performance
PLOP	present level of performance
PT	physical therapy/therapist

Acronym	Stands for
PTI	parent training and information
RTI	Response to Intervention
SL(P)	speech language (pathologist)
SPP	state performance plan
STO	short-term objective
TAT	teacher assistance team
USDE	U.S. Department of Education
VR	vocational rehabilitation

Common Special Education Terms Defined

Not all of the words you'll hear are acronyms. Some of them are terms that have a very specific meaning when used in regard to education. Not all states define terms exactly the same way, but there are some terms that have common meaning across the board.

Accommodations

Accommodations refer to the adjustments to how your child is taught to help him participate in his general education class. You may also hear these referred to as "modifications." Accommodations can take many forms, including changes to the format in which your child is taught, the amount of time he has to take tests and complete work, behavioral intervention plans, and supportive technology or other services.

FACT

Accommodations don't change what your child is being taught or tested on; they just change the way that information is presented to him.

Adequate Yearly Progress (AYP)

Adequate yearly progress is how much your state's education department expects kids to learn in each subject area each year. Though states may define adequate yearly progress differently, as many states have adopted the Common Core State Standards, it's starting to become more standardized.

QUESTION

What are the Common Core State Standards?
The Common Core State Standards (CCSS) are a set of defined expectations for grades K-12 in reading, writing, language, listening, and mathematics. They were created to make sure that students across the nation are equally prepared for college or the workforce upon graduation from high school. Although CCSS is voluntary, forty-five states have adopted them.

If your child has a special education plan, she may be working on academic goals at a different rate and not meet the adequate yearly progress as defined by your state's standards. As long as her personal educational goals are being addressed and met, this is not a problem.

Americans with Disabilities Act (ADA)

The Americans with Disabilities Act is a federal civil rights law that says people with disabilities cannot be discriminated against when it comes to accessibility, employment, transportation, and other public accommodations. That is, it makes sure that people with disabilities are able to get to services and have the same rights as a person without disabilities. ADA is not limited to schools; it provides protection in the larger community as well.

Assistive Technology (AT)

Assistive technology is any type of device that is used to help a child with a disability be more functional in a certain area. Often, you'll hear about assistive technology used to help nonverbal children communicate with teachers and caregivers, but assistive technology is not limited to communication. Children who have learning disabilities in reading and writing may use some sort of assistive technology to help make those areas easier for them, just as children with physical disabilities may use assistive equipment to improve other types of functioning.

Behavioral Assessment (BA)

You may more frequently hear this term as a "functional behavioral assessment (FBA)." In either case, it refers to the process of gathering and analyzing information about your child's behavior. That information can then be used in creating a plan to help your child and his teachers manage unwanted or inappropriate behaviors.

ESSENTIAL

A good functional behavioral assessment consists of data gathered through direct observation; teacher and parental input; and observations of how often, for how long, and under what circumstances a behavior occurs.

Behavioral/Behavior Disorders (BD)

This can be a scary term for a parent to hear, particularly because the word *disorder* often implies a condition that is chronic and persistent. In some states, the phrase is used in regard to children who show inappropriate behaviors and trouble with social interaction that get in the way of learning.

Behavior Intervention Plan (BIP)

A behavior intervention plan is a plan developed by your child's team to help her learn and maintain appropriate behavior and social skills. Ideally, a plan should be positive and proactive as opposed to containing only negative consequences and reactive solutions.

Child Find (CF)

Child Find is a federal program outlined in IDEA that requires every state to locate (or "find") children from birth to age twenty-one who have disabilities or who are at risk of developmental disabilities. Because Child Find has a strong focus on children who have not yet entered school, it's usually tied into early intervention and kindergarten screenings. The program relies on professionals and parents making referrals; despite the name, nobody actually goes door-to-door to find kids with disabilities.

Consent or Prior Written Consent

This is a crucial term for parents to know, since it's a right you have when it comes to assessment, evaluation, and placement of your child for special education services. In almost all cases, a school cannot evaluate, change your child's placement, or provide services without your written consent.

Comprehensive Educational Evaluation

A comprehensive educational evaluation is comprised of the assessments, observations, and testing performed by your child's school to see if he has a disability. IDEA says that a comprehensive educational evaluation has to be done before a child is found eligible for special education. After the evaluation is complete, you and your child's team members should sit down at a meeting to discuss the results.

Developmental Disability or Developmental Delay (DD)

A developmental disability is a physical or mental condition that impairs your child's ability to learn or gain skills at the same rate as other children her age. Many younger children who receive early intervention services are classified as being "developmentally delayed" because it is not always apparent what is causing the delay.

Due Process

Due process is another important term to know as a parent. It's the outlined procedure for resolving disputes between parents and special education agencies. For children between the ages of birth and three, it's the process by which you can resolve a dispute about how early intervention services are being provided. If you have a school-aged child, due process is what you would follow if you and the school district were unable to agree on your child's eligibility for services, the results of an evaluation, or your child's program and placement.

Due Process Hearing (and Due Process Officer)

The due process hearing is the actual legal meeting at which a trained, neutral party (the due process officer) hears and looks at all the evidence related to the issue about which you and the school district disagree. It's a lot like a court hearing in that a full record of the proceedings is kept and the hearing officer presents a written decision after considering all the evidence.

Early Intervention (EI)

Early intervention services are the services provided to children ages birth to three who have a developmental delay, a known disorder that causes delays in development, or who are at risk for delays. Though early intervention is provided for in IDEA, the types of services and goals are different than special education services for school-aged children.

Extended School Year (ESY)

Usually when you hear about ESY, it's accompanied by the phrase "services," as in "extended school year services." Extended school year services are special education and related services that are provided during summer vacation or other long periods of time when there is no school.

FACT

Not all children who are eligible for special education are eligible for ESY. It's a decision your child's team must make based on whether or not your child will continue to make progress or maybe even lose skills without year-round services.

Inclusion

Inclusion is a concept that goes by many names, including *mainstreaming* and *integration*. You may hear the terms "inclusion" or "full inclusion" when your child's special education placement is being discussed. It refers to including your child in a regular education classroom for some of his learning. Many schools try to make sure kids are fully included in the general education classroom, adding either an extra person or other supports for your child, but the level of inclusion really depends on a child's individual needs.

Individualized Education Program (IEP)

The IEP is the cornerstone of your child's special education program. It's the written plan that includes—among other things—information about how he is currently performing in school, his specialized educational goals, and what services and accommodations he needs to meet those goals, and it specifies which team members are responsible for working on each goal.

Individual Family Service Plan (IFSP)

Individual family service plans are not unlike IEPs; they are written plans outlining the services for children ages birth to three. Early interventions services are designed to not only meet the needs of the child but also the needs of the family, so the plan is family centered as opposed to educationally oriented.

Intellectual Disability

This term refers to the limitations in mental functioning of a child with cognitive disabilities or what is sometimes referred to as "mental retardation." A child with an intellectual disability will often have difficulties not only in learning but in daily living skills as well. The level of difficulty is dependent on the severity of the disability.

FACT

The term *intellectual disability* replaced the term *mental retardation* when Rosa's Law was signed in October 2010, though many people still use "mental retardation" because it's more widely understood. The meaning is the same; it's just the phrase that is different.

Least Restrictive Environment (LRE)

Although the concept of least restrictive environment is simple, in practice it's often a hot button at meetings. The LRE is the placement or special education program for your child that gives her the best chance of learning with peers who do not have disabilities.

ESSENTIAL

The range of learning environments is wide and open to interpretation, and there is no one "right" least restrictive environment (LRE). Your child's least restrictive environment is determined by her team and is based on her specific educational needs and abilities.

Mainstream(ing)

A mainstream classroom is a regular education classroom taught by a regular education teacher as opposed to a special education teacher. Mainstreaming refers to the process of including a child who receives special education services in the regular classroom for instruction. The parameters for how long and with what supports a child is mainstreamed are determined by his IEP team and written into the IEP document.

The No Child Left Behind Act (NCLB)

You will often hear the No Child Left Behind Act referred to as "nickelbee." It's a complicated and controversial federal law that was reauthorized in 2001 as the Elementary and Secondary Education Act (ESEA). Its main goal is to provide better educational opportunities for at-risk students, some of whom qualify for special education, and some who do not. The act says that each state and its school districts need to be able to measure the educational progress of all students. It has a complex federal funding structure based on how well or how poorly schools perform.

ALERT

One of the main controversies is that NCLB requires the entire student body to achieve the same level of academic success, which is not always possible for students with special education needs.

Present Levels of Academic Achievement and Functional Performance (PLAFFP)

This portion of your child's IEP describes her strengths, weaknesses, the way she learns, and at what level she is currently performing academically. This statement is also sometimes referred to as a PLOP (present level of performance) or a PLEP (present level of educational performance). Whatever it's called, the information comes from evaluations, assessments, and observations.

Related Services

As discussed in Chapter 1, related services are services that are needed for your child to be able to learn successfully. They include, but are not limited to, occupational therapy, assistive technology, physical therapy, and counseling. In some cases, related services may be all your child needs in terms of special education.

Response to Intervention (RTI)

Response to Intervention is a process by which students having trouble in school can get extra help without being in a special education program. There are very specific rules for how it must be carried out, and just because your child participates in response-to-intervention programs doesn't exclude him from being eligible for special education. For some students, these interventions may be all they need to catch up to their peers.

§ (Section)

This isn't exactly a term, and it isn't limited to special education. If your child is going through the special education process or receives services, it's a symbol you'll see often. It is a sign that means "section," and it is used to designate the place in a legal document in which certain information can be found. Since IDEA is the legal document that governs special education, you can assume this symbol is being used to refer to the supporting rule or section of IDEA unless otherwise noted.

Student Assistance Team (SAT) or Pupil Assistance Team (PAT)

The student assistance team is sometimes known as a "prereferral team." It's a group of educators within a school or school district to whom a teacher can turn for advice for classroom interventions that may help your child before looking at a referral for special education services.

In some school districts, the student assistance team also is available to sit down with you, your child, and the classroom teacher to come up with a written plan of action for how to address the difficulties your child is having.

CHAPTER 3

A Quick Look at Special Education Law

You don't have to be lawyer to make sure your child gets the right services in place, but you do need to know a little about the different laws that are relevant to kids with disabilities. If you're not familiar with the laws, it's very possible that something can happen in a meeting that you don't understand or that your child may not be given all the accommodations he deserves. Unfortunately, you can't always count on the school district to explain in detail all the different laws that apply to your child. It's not always a deliberate attempt to deny your child services. Many schools expect you to speak up if you don't understand something or forget that parents aren't as knowledgeable as professionals who deal with this material all the time.

The Americans with Disabilities Act Amendments Act of 2008 (ADA)

Strangely, one of the laws under which you might find your child has protection isn't really a law dealing with special education at all. The Americans with Disabilities Act was first signed into law in 1990 but was updated in 2008, changing it from the easily pronounced acronym, ADA, to the current mouthful of ADAAA. Even with the changes made to the law in 2008, most people still refer to it as ADA.

What Is ADA?

As noted before, ADA is not a special education law; it's a civil rights law that provides some basic protections to everyone with disabilities, not just children. It gives a three-part definition of what, under the law, is considered to be a disability. Under ADA, a person has a disability if he has:

- a physical or mental impairment that significantly limits the ability to participate in a major life activity; or
- a record of that type of impairment; or
- is seen as having that type of impairment.

As you can see, the definition of "disability" under ADA is sort of open to interpretation, and there isn't an accompanying list of disabilities that qualify. This is very different than in special education law. That doesn't mean that your child can't benefit from ADA, though.

The Purpose of ADA

The basic purpose of this act is to "prohibit discrimination solely on the basis of disability in employment, public services, and accommodations." In simpler terms, if a child or an adult has a disability that is recognized under the criteria of the law, nobody can tell him he can't have a job or participate in public services just because of his disability. If he has a physical disability, then public places are supposed to have accommodations such as being wheelchair-friendly or providing Braille menus.

FACT

Not all public places are ADA compliant. To some degree that's because the law didn't provide any federal funding to help with renovations, and some businesses simply can't afford to make the changes. If an organization has less then twelve employees, it can be exempted from ADA compliance.

ADA's Connection to Special Education

If your child has a disability that affects her when you're out and about in the world, then ADA provides some peace of mind that the community can't legally discriminate against her. But does this have any bearing when it comes to her education?

Like most things in special education, there's not really a simple yes or no answer to that question. ADA doesn't come into effect as a way to *get* your child special education services in a public school system, but it does combine with other laws to provide your child with some additional protections. For example:

> *Jennifer, a high school student, has cerebral palsy. She does not have any learning disabilities, but her mobility is impaired to the point that she uses a wheelchair. This year, Jennifer would like to attend a program at a regional vocational high school, a program that is available to all high school students and to which students are transported by bus from the regular high school. The bus that is provided is not wheelchair accessible, and the program she wants to attend is on the second floor of the vocational school, but the school does not have an elevator.*

In this case, Jennifer's ability to participate in her education is limited, but her rights are protected under ADA in two ways. Since the vocational high school is considered a job-training program, it is required to make sure that everyone with disabilities is able to participate. ADA also says that schools need to make "reasonable accommodations" for eligible students, including, but not limited to, providing an accessible location and transportation.

Jennifer's parents can legally argue that her civil rights are being violated by the school district if it does not provide special transportation and a way to physically access the vocational program in which she is enrolled.

Section 504 of the Rehabilitation Act of 1973

While its official name is Section 504 of the Rehabilitation Act of 1973, you'll probably only ever hear this law referred to as Section 504. It's actually more likely that you'll hear things like "Does your child have a 504 plan or an IEP?" or "Can he get services under 504?" Like the Americans with Disabilities Act, Section 504 is a law that provides protection to all people with disabilities, not just school-age children.

The Purpose of Section 504

Section 504 is a civil rights law that predates both IDEA and ADA and is significantly different from both of them. The Americans with Disabilities Act is designed to prevent widespread discrimination. The Individuals with Disabilities in Education Act is designed to outline how schools deal with special education. Section 504 makes it illegal for programs or activities that get federal funding from the U.S Department of Education to discriminate against people with disabilities.

As you can imagine, Section 504 covers a whole lot of programs, including public schools of all levels. In fact, because Section 504 came before IDEA, it is actually the first law that specifically required schools to provide "appropriate" educational services for students with disabilities. It's not as clearly spelled out as in IDEA, but under Section 504 a public school has to provide "reasonable" accommodations to make sure a student with a disability gets the same benefit from his *regular* education as his nondisabled peers.

Section 504's Connection to Special Education

Section 504 sounds as though it requires the same things of a school as IDEA does, but that's not actually the case. It can be challenging for both parents and school districts to understand how Section 504 differs from IDEA when it comes to education. There are a few things to know that can make it a little easier.

- Section 504 was signed into law before IDEA was even an idea, let alone a law, which means there is some overlap in what both laws require schools to provide for children with disabilities.
- As a civil rights law that applies to people of all ages, Section 504 defines disability the same way ADA defines it—having a physical or mental impairment (or record of one) that majorly affects life activities.
- Section 504 is not specific to special education; accommodations and modifications provided under Section 504 are to help your child in a regular education program, not a special education program.
- IDEA is specific to special education, so it has considerably more detail about what defines a disability that can affect learning. It also defines how a school has to evaluate for those disabilities, and spells out specific categories of disability that allow your child to get special education services.

QUESTION

If my child has a diagnosed disability, why doesn't he automatically qualify for special education services?
IDEA 2004 defines a disability as being "educationally handicapping," or interfering with your child's ability to learn. This is different than a medical or clinical diagnosis or even from how Section 504 defines disability. You will have to prove your child's disability affects learning before he qualifies for special education.

If your child has a diagnosed disability that affects major life activities, like self-care, walking, hearing, seeing, breathing, speaking, and/or learning, but doesn't fit into the strict criteria outlined by IDEA 2004, he may be able to receive help in school under Section 504.

IDEA 2004

IDEA 2004 is the most recent version of the law that was originally passed in 1975. Each time Congress has looked at the law again, or "reauthorized" it, there have been changes made to special education rules, regulations, and procedures. When IDEA was reauthorized in 2004, there were some major changes made to it, changes that clarified the procedures an educational agency needs to follow and in regard to the programs for which a state can use federal special education funds.

Your Child's "Free Appropriate Public Education"

You already know that your child is entitled to a "free appropriate public education," or a FAPE. That FAPE may be free to you, but it's not really free, and sometimes that can get in the way of your child getting the services she needs.

ESSENTIAL

Every state is required to put into effect all of the pieces of IDEA 2004, including all of the screening programs, early intervention services, school-based intervention services, and special education services. As long as a state is sticking to the rules of IDEA 2004, the federal government provides money to help fund special education programs.

Federal funding doesn't come close to covering the cost of implementing IDEA 2004, which means state and local educational agencies often have trouble covering the costs of special education. This, in turn, can put local schools in a tough position when it comes to actually providing all the pieces your child needs to have a FAPE. While that's the reality, legally, it's not really your problem.

ALERT

Your child's IEP is determined by her needs, not the money the school has available. If you are told "there isn't money for that," and the team agrees your child needs the service, let the school know you are aware that services cannot be decided as a part of a budget.

History of IDEA 2004

Over the years, IDEA has evolved quite a bit. What started out as a law to define the educational rights of school-aged children with disabilities has developed into a highly detailed and refined law that outlines procedures, regulations, and the rights and responsibilities of parents and school districts alike.

IDEA 2004 lists categories of disabilities, including specific learning disabilities that children may have that can affect their learning. The law also specifies that children who have not yet reached school age can receive special education services, known as early intervention services.

IDEA 2004 also works to make special education more closely aligned with regular education by using some of the same phrases and concepts found in the No Child Left Behind Act, a law that outlines academic achievement for nondisabled students.

Goals of IDEA 2004

Making sure children with disabilities have the same opportunity to participate in school and society as other kids was one of the major goals when IDEA was reauthorized in 2004.

FACT

IDEA 2004 defines a disability very differently than ADA and Section 504. In part it says: "Disability is a natural part of the human experience and in no way diminishes the right of individuals to participate in or contribute to society." (IDEA, Sec. 601)

Making sure that children with disabilities have the tools they need to be equal participants was just one of the goals of IDEA 2004. It also set out to make sure that:

- Educational programs are monitored to gauge how effective they are in meeting the individual needs of children with disabilities.
- Undiagnosed disabilities don't get in the way of a child's success in education.
- Children with disabilities are getting the services they need from public schools for a FAPE.
- Parents of children with disabilities know their rights and that those rights are protected.
- State and local educational agencies have the money they need for special education services.

These goals and the subsequent changes in IDEA 2004 make it easier for parents to be a big part of the special education process. It also makes it more difficult for schools to change your child's IEP or to not provide the program and services specified on your child's IEP.

Parts A, B, C, and D

There are four main sections of IDEA 2004: Parts A and B, Part C, and Part D. Parts A and B are usually talked about together because they are the two sections that cover special education for children between the ages of three and twenty-one years old. Together, the sections cover all of the rules, regulations, and procedures for determining eligibility for services as well as the required and related services.

Part C is the section of IDEA 2004 that spells out the procedures and services for infants and toddlers with or at risk for disabilities, also known as early intervention. As you will read in Chapter 4, this part of the law is very different from Parts A, B, and D.

Part D of the law deals with funding for national programs and/or activities that can help make educational services for children with disabilities better. The purpose of Part D is to give educational agencies some guidance as to how they can use special education funding to make their systems work better. For example, Part D allows for federal funding for research, staff training, parent training, technology, and other ways of providing information about the best practices in special education and early intervention.

A Side-by-Side Comparison of the Laws

Understanding how ADA, IDEA 2004, and Section 504 work together can help you be a more informed advocate to ensure your child is getting a Free and Appropriate Public Education. Here's a look at your child's rights under each law.

▼ A SIDE-BY-SIDE COMPARISON OF ADA, IDEA 2004, AND SECTION 504

About the Law	ADA	IDEA 2004	Section 504
Who does it cover/ protect?	ADA covers all persons with disabilities that greatly limit major life activities. Persons must be qualified for the program or job in question.	Children (3–21) found eligible under one of the thirteen categories of disability and need special education and/or related services.	All persons with disabilities that greatly limit major life activities like self-care, walking, hearing, seeing, breathing, speaking, and/ or learning.
What is its purpose?	ADA is a civil rights law that prohibits discrimination of persons with disabilities in the realms of employment, accommodations, and public services.	IDEA 2004 is federal statute that provides rules, regulations, and procedures to ensure a free and appropriate education to covered children with disabilities.	Section 504 is a far-reaching civil rights law protecting the rights of all persons with disabilities in any program that receives federal funds. It intends to make sure such persons can participate as much like nondisabled peers as possible.
What does it say about FAPE?	ADA does not address FAPE but can be combined with Section 504 mandates to ensure that a child receives a FAPE via reasonable accommodations.	A "free appropriate public education" is at the heart of IDEA 2004, and is defined as "specially designed instruction at no cost to parents, to meet the unique needs of a child with a disability." This means special education for qualified children.	Section 504 provides for an "appropriate" education that allows students with disabilities to have the same educational experience as nondisabled peers. With such a broad definition, this means qualified children may receive help in the regular classroom or special education services as a team deems necessary to help him access his regular education.

About the Law	ADA	IDEA 2004	Section 504
What type of federal funding is provided?	No funding is specifically provided, though there are agencies that provide grants to help with training and other assistance.	IDEA 2004 mandates federal funding be provided to help state and local educational units meet the requirements of providing services to infants, toddlers, and school-age children with disabilities.	No federal funds are provided. It is the responsibility of the state and local schools to fund services.
Special education versus regular education	ADA does not speak to the type of education. It requires public institutions to provide reasonable accommodations for persons with disabilities. These can include specialized equipment, alternative testing format or presentation, and accessibility to physical locations.	IDEA 2004 provides special education and related services to help children get the full benefit of the regular education curriculum.	Section 504 usually supports learning in the regular education classroom. The law requires that schools provide assistance to eliminate any barriers that are in the way of a student being able to be a full participant in regular education curriculum.
How is evaluation/ placement handled?	Not applicable.	IDEA 2004 requires a comprehensive educational evaluation prior to eligibility/ placement. Eligibility for special education services is based on how the evaluative data and reports from people who work with the children and parents fit IDEA 2004 standards. Parental consent is required for evaluation and placement.	Section 504 recommends, but does not require, schools to get parent consent before evaluation. Placement/ program decisions are made in the same way as with IDEA 2004, but Section 504 requires students to be taught in the regular education classrooms with nondisabled peers as much as reasonably possible.

About the Law	ADA	IDEA 2004	Section 504
Procedural safeguards? (rights)	ADA does not have specific procedural safeguards for parents and/or children with disabilities.	IDEA 2004 requires prior written notice to parents before referral for evaluation, prior to determination of eligibility, placement, and change of services. If a child has behavioral issues, a functional behavior assessment and a behavioral intervention plan has to be written to help teach and reinforce appropriate behavior. At all times, due process rights must be followed.	Section 504 only requires prior written notice to parents if there is to be a "significant change" in a child's placement. IDEA 2004 due process rights apply if a child is referred for evaluation for special educations services and the child's team decides not to evaluate.
How are complaints handled?	Under ADA, complaints must be filed with the Office of Civil Rights or the court system, though these systems often encourage parents and schools to try mediation before formal legal action.	IDEA 2004 provides very specific procedures for dealing with complaints in regard to eligibility, evaluation, services, and/or how an IEP is implemented. These procedures include filing formal complaints, mediated resolution sessions, and due process hearings.	Section 504 provides for hearings in the case of disagreement about identification, evaluation, and placement. Parents have the right to have an attorney at the hearing. After that, Section 504 does not specify a next-step process, but it does encourage state and local agencies to create their own policies in this regard.
Who is the overseeing/ enforcing agency?	The U.S. Office of Civil Rights	Each individual state's Department of Education and the U.S. Office of Special Education Programs	The U.S. Office of Civil Rights

CHAPTER 4

A Look at Early Intervention Services

Part C of IDEA 2004 is all about early intervention (EI) services. If your child is already of school age, and her disability was identified before she went to school, you may have already participated in early intervention services. They are designed to help children ages birth to three years old who are experiencing or are at risk for delays in gaining or maintaining basic developmental skills.

Do All States Provide Early Intervention Services?

Part C is a discretionary program, which means that money the federal government provides to each state to help support the program isn't a set amount each year, and each state has some flexibility in how it runs its EI programs.

All states have to identify an agency that will receive the money and run the program. In some states, this agency is part of the Department of Education, while in others it is part of the Department of Health and Human Services. Regardless of which agency is responsible, that agency has to assure that services are available to all eligible children and families before the federal government will provide money to help.

ALERT

A big difference between special education services for school-age children and Part C is that early intervention services don't have to be free. Your state can charge on a sliding fee scale, or, in some states, your child's insurance company may be billed for some of her services.

The amount of money each state receives is based on a formula that takes into account the number of children in the birth-to-three age range that have been identified with disabilities or the need for EI. Federal funding is also dependent on your state meeting other criteria about procedures for identifying children with or at risk for disabilities, and other administrative details outlined in IDEA 2004.

Identifying Children Who Need Early Intervention

One of the things IDEA expects states to do for early intervention is to make sure they are conducting what's known as "Child Find" activities. Basically this means that early intervention services agencies need to let parents know that services are available, and they must have a referral system in place for children who are suspected to have disabilities.

One big part of Child Find is that health-care workers and childcare workers are often trained to look for signs of delays and make a referral based on their concerns. If your child was born with a genetic disorder that is known to cause development delays—such as Down syndrome—or a physical disability that is associated with delays or difficulties—such as a cleft palate—the hospital will often make a direct referral to the early intervention agency to get the process started when your child is born.

FACT

Parental permission (or *consent*) is not required to make a referral for early intervention. However, you must give consent before your child can be assessed or evaluated. You do have the right to refuse if you don't want your child to be evaluated.

Sometimes, though, delays aren't noticeable until your child is a little older and not meeting his developmental milestones as expected. In that case, your pediatrician or childcare provider may notice it and have some concerns. Ideally, whoever has concerns will speak with you about what was noticed and let you know that a referral for your child for evaluation for early intervention services is warranted, but sometimes a pediatrician or provider will make the referral directly. You can also self-refer to the early intervention agency by calling, expressing your concerns about your child's development, and asking that your child be evaluated.

The Assessment Process

Once your child has been referred, the process varies from state to state. Some states perform a basic screening of skills to see if there are areas of concern that need to be evaluated in more depth, and some states will go right to a formal evaluation process. The difference is that a screening is a less formal assessment of your child's overall skills. Early intervention (EI) professionals will use basic screening tools or observation to get a sense of what types of skills your child is having trouble with, then decide what type of specialized evaluation your child needs.

For example, if your toddler doesn't use words to communicate but has no trouble with other skills, the EI agency may refer him for an audiology test to make sure his hearing is okay and for an evaluation with a speech-language pathologist, a professional who specializes in communication development.

ESSENTIAL

Once your child is referred for early intervention, the agency has forty-five days in which to complete the evaluation process and hold an initial meeting to determine eligibility. Practically speaking, since you have to give consent to evaluate, the clock often starts when you sign a Consent to Evaluate form.

Whether your state begins with a screening or goes right to evaluation, there are five basic areas of development that are looked at to see if your child may have developmental delays or a disability. They are:

1. **Physical development:** Physical development includes vision, hearing, gross motor skills, and fine motor skills. Gross motor skills are those that use the larger muscles in your child's body to help with basic developmental milestones such as rolling over, sitting up, crawling, and walking. Gross motor skills are affected by muscle tone and strength. Fine motor skills use the small muscles to help with tasks like grasping things, speech, and picking up and manipulating objects. Delays in fine motor skills can affect a number of different areas of development.

2. **Cognitive development:** Cognitive development refers to your infant or toddler's ability to think, learn, and problem-solve as she begins to makes sense of her surroundings. Between the ages of birth and three, your child's cognitive development should help her meet such developmental milestones as paying attention to faces and recognizing the familiar people in her life, being curious about the world around her and trying to interact with it, being able to follow simple directions, and identifying the purpose of everyday objects.

3. **Communication development:** Communication development is your child's ability to use language to express her needs and emotions, as

well as her ability to understand the use of language. There are a number of developmental milestones to watch out for in the realm of communication, including babbling, responding to sounds and her name, imitating sounds and communicative actions (such as shaking your head no), and, eventually, using recognizable words.

4. **Social/emotional development:** Social and emotional development is harder to gauge, as it develops more slowly. It involves your child's ability to play, feel happy and secure, make friends, express and recognize emotions (including empathy), use basic conflict resolution skills, and just enjoying being around other people. Typical milestones in this area include spontaneous smiling, stranger anxiety, throwing temper tantrums, and beginning to play at first near, and then with, other children.

5. **Adaptive behavior development:** Adaptive behaviors are those that allow your child to gain independence in self-care and everyday life. Infant and toddler adaptive development includes such skills as being able to hold and drink from a bottle/cup, self-feeding (with fingers at first and then with utensils), being able to get dressed, toilet training, and other basic hygiene skills.

Your child will be evaluated by a team of professionals, each of whom is a specialist in one or more of these areas of development. Often the evaluation team will come to your home to be able to observe your child in her familiar environment. You will be asked numerous questions about her development, your concerns, and your family life. It may feel too personal, but the more information the EI team can gather, the more able they are to determine if your child has delays or developmental needs that aren't being met.

After the Assessment

Once all the evaluations have been completed, the EI agency will look over the reports and information to determine whether your child meets your state's guidelines for services and/or definition of "developmentally disabled." Either way, you will get a notice informing you of the decision. If your child is not found eligible, you should receive a copy of the evaluation results and a notice explaining why your child is not eligible for services.

If my child isn't eligible for early intervention services, does that mean she doesn't have a developmental delay or disability?
Your child may show signs of developmental delays or a disability and still not be found eligible for services because her delays don't meet the criteria for EI services in your state.

If your child is found ineligible for services, you have a few options. The first, and most important, is to sit down with a representative of the EI agency who can explain to you exactly what your child's test results mean and why she does not qualify for services. Then:

- **Ask for recommendations of how you can help your child.** Sometimes your child may not meet the criteria for EI services, but services like speech or occupational therapy are covered by her insurance if your pediatrician makes a referral. In other cases, the EI agency might be able to provide you with some information about how to work with her at home or refer you to another agency that can help.
- **Set up an appointment for your child to be rescreened in six months.** As time goes by, if your child's skills don't improve, she will be more likely to qualify for services because she will be that much further behind her peers. It's not an ideal situation, but keeping track of where she is developmentally will help her in the long run.
- **File a formal complaint or dispute if you strongly disagree with the agency's denial of services.** You should be given a handbook that outlines your parental rights and procedural safeguards every time you meet with the EI agency. That handout explains the process that your state follows for handling disputes.
- **Contact a disability rights advocate or parents rights organization if you need support in the process.** You have the right to bring any support person with you to any meeting at any time.

Your special education rights as a parent and the procedures that need to be followed by the state you live in are explained in a handout or booklet that you should receive at every IEP meeting. It goes by different names in different states, but it should be something close to the following: *Parental Rights and Procedural Safeguards, Notice of Procedural Safeguards, Parents' Notice of Procedural Safeguards,* or *Procedural Safeguards Notice.*

Writing an Individual Family Service Plan

If your child *is* found eligible for service, a meeting will be scheduled to sit down, go over all the information, and write an individual family service plan (IFSP) to provide services for your child and family. The IFSP is the document that details your child's strengths and weaknesses, his current skill level, what services he needs to improve those skills, as well any services you might need to learn how to work with him at home.

IFSP versus an IEP

The main difference between an IFSP and an IEP is that an IFSP focuses on the needs of the entire family in helping your child's developmental skills, while an IEP is focused on the educational needs of your child. Remember, special education for the school-age child is there to help him access a public education like his peers, while early intervention services are designed to help young children with disabilities or developmental delays gain skills.

The reasoning for including the family in the services on an IFSP is simple: A typical infant and toddler spends the majority of his time with a caregiver, so it's the caregiver who will spend the most time working with him to improve his skills. A few hours a week of specialized therapy can only help so much—you, as your child's parent or caregiver, need to continue practicing those skills and engaging your child at home to keep gaining ground.

The IFSP Team

When you sit down to develop your child's IFSP, there is a whole team of people who will be involved. As your child starts going to various developmental therapies, the team will grow to include the therapists who are working with him, but initially the IFSP team may be relatively small.

The team consists of you (your child's parents or guardians), any family or caregivers you think should be involved in the early intervention process, a family advocate or outside case worker (if you have or requested one), the service coordinator assigned to your child by the EI agency, the professionals who evaluated your child, and, under some circumstances, the people who will be providing services to your child.

ESSENTIAL

A service coordinator is like a case manager. She will be the one to find professionals to provide services for your child, coordinate transportation, oversee progress and problems, and hold and lead meetings. She is your single point of contact when it comes to questions or concerns.

The tricky part about having service providers participate in the initial meeting is that the services your child will receive are supposed to be a team decision. That means that although your child's service coordinator may have an idea of what your child might need for assistance and qualifies for, none of those services are truly official until the IFSP team is in agreement they are necessary.

Writing the IFSP

Under the law, you must have at least seven days *prior written notice* before the scheduled meeting. That means the EI agency has to make sure you get a notification in the mail at least seven calendar days before the date of the meeting. You do have the right to waive prior written notice if you have the opportunity to have the meeting sooner. You just have to sign a waiver form at the meeting saying that you didn't have prior written notice and you are agreeable to that.

As long as all the members of the IFSP team can be there, you don't anticipate any difficulty in your child being found eligible, and you don't feel like you need more time to research or prepare for the meeting, you're not losing anything by waiving that right. Just make sure you sign the paper!

The team will discuss and write an IFSP at this meeting. The IFSP has to have certain information in it, including:

- Your child's current level of development in the five skill areas
- Your worries about your child's development and how you prioritize those concerns
- The resources you have to be able to implement the IFSP and what's known as any "barriers to service," which are stumbling blocks that would make it hard for you to follow the IFSP. These might be something as simple as not having transportation to get your child to a service provider's office or as complicated as your child having two homes, one of which is not willing to participate in your child's EI program.
- The desired outcomes for your child. Essentially, these are statements of what skills the team would like your child to improve upon or acquire and the measurable steps that will be taken to make that happen.
- The services that are needed to address those outcomes and type of service provider who will be working with your child (such as a speech therapist, an occupational therapist, an early interventionist, etc.) to meet those outcomes.
- Where services will take place, which IDEA says should be provided in your child's *natural environment* "to the maximum extent possible." If your child is at home with you, the natural environment is home. If your child is in a daycare or preschool, that's a community-based natural environment. If services are not going to be provided in the natural environment, then the service coordinator needs to include an explanation of why in the IFSP.

Once the IFSP is written, you have to give written permission for each service before it can begin. You don't have to agree to all the services, and if you agree to one and not another, it doesn't mean your child can't get any services at all. You also have the right to take back permission for any service at any time.

After the Plan Is Written

After your child's IFSP is written, services will begin as soon as possible. Your service coordinator will be arranging for providers to work with your child and is available to answer your questions. Six months after the plan is written (and every six months thereafter), there will be a review meeting to check in on your child's progress. Should there be any proposed changes in services at a six-month review, the EI agency is required to provide you with prior written notice of the proposed changes.

For example, if your child's speech therapist thinks he's progressing well enough to cut down to one day a week from two, you have to be notified of that idea before the meeting. The law also says that the IFSP team needs to meet annually to look at your child's plan to see whether he's met any of his goals, and to write new goals or revise the current ones.

Transitioning to School-Based Services

Once your child turns three, she will no longer receive services under Part C and will transition to Part B, meaning she'll now have an IEP and school-based services. Practically, what that means is that your child's developmental delay or disability is now looked at from an "educationally handicapping" perspective instead of an early intervention perspective. That means that at least ninety days before your child's third birthday, your service coordinator will hold a transition meeting to help create a plan of how to make a smooth adjustment from early intervention services to Part B services. That transition and what services will look like varies drastically from state to state.

Your local public school district will be notified and provided with your contact information, as they are the agency responsible for Part B services. It is then their responsibility to provide you with your *Parental Rights and Procedural Safeguards* under IDEA, decide whether your child is eligible for services under Part B (or have your child evaluated to help make the decision), and then sit down with all involved parties to write an IEP.

Since your child's services need to be educationally based, ideally the programs available to your child include preschool services, early education programs, or Head Start, but in some states there is no preschool program available. Luckily, IDEA also provides for "other appropriate services."

It's a confusing concept, but it gives the school district and the EI agency some leeway in providing services to help your child be able to learn at the same rate as a nondevelopmentally disabled peer if they were both in a school setting. In fact, in some states, the local education agency partners with the EI agency to continue providing services for children three to five years of age, after which time there's an official transition-to-public-school meeting.

CHAPTER 5

The Thirteen Categories of Disability

If your child is eligible for special education services under IDEA, it's because she has a disability that is affecting her learning. IDEA defines thirteen categories of disability; your child must meet the definition of one of them to be eligible for special education. This doesn't mean there are only thirteen disabilities that special education can address—the categories are broad enough that a number of different types of disabling conditions are included under each heading.

What to Know about "Disabling Conditions" and "Adverse Effect"

Once your child has transitioned to Part B or is being evaluated for special education services in the public school, there are thirteen categories of disability, or disabling conditions, under which he might be found eligible for services. There are a few important points to keep in mind when you're looking at the categories of disabilities:

- Just having one of the defined "disabling conditions" doesn't automatically qualify your child for services; the disability also needs to have an "adverse effect" on his education. Basically, that means even if you can show your child has a disability, you also have to show that it's causing enough problems with his learning that he needs special education.
- IDEA defines the categories of disability and uses the language "adverse effect," but what adverse effect means is open to interpretation. With some disabilities, it's very clear that educational performance is being affected, but with others, like some learning disabilities, emotional problems, and even high-functioning autism, it's not as clear. That can often cause a lot of debate and problems between schools and parents.
- If your child is being transitioned in from early intervention services, IDEA gives states the leeway to keep the label of "developmental delay" until your child turns nine. This is a good move because some disabilities aren't as easy to diagnose when your child is younger, and it cuts down on the possibility of misdiagnosis. Just make sure to ask your school system if your state has taken advantage of this option.

Autism

In the past decade, the numbers of diagnosed cases of autism have increased substantially. In March 2013, the Centers for Disease Control and Prevention reported that close to one out of fifty children between the ages of six and seventeen has autism. Currently, autism is one of five subcategories of disorders that together are known as pervasive developmental disorders. The others are childhood disintegrative disorder (also known as Heller's syndrome), Asperger syndrome, Rett syndrome, and pervasive developmental disorder, not otherwise specified (PDD, NOS).

ESSENTIAL

The latest edition of the *Diagnostic and Statistical Manual of Mental Disorders*, the *DSM-5*, has changed the criteria for autism and eliminated the subcategories as diagnoses. As of 2104, all children who meet the defined criteria will be diagnosed as having an autism spectrum disorder, with a support level of 1, 2, or 3.

What Are the Characteristics of Autism?

The autism spectrum is very broad, so children who have autism can have very different symptoms and very different abilities. If your child has Autism Spectrum Disorder: Level 1 (currently known as Asperger syndrome), he's not as likely to have difficulties with intelligence or his own verbal communication as he is likely to have difficulty with the other abilities affected by this neurological disorder. If your child is on the other end of the autism spectrum, it's possible that he isn't able to talk, has difficulty learning, and isn't as likely to relate to other people in a typical way. For the purpose of special education needs and eligibility, the Individuals with Disabilities Education Act (IDEA) looks at three main characteristics of autism that can affect learning:

1. **Impaired communication.** Kids who have an autism spectrum disorder typically have some trouble with communication, but how that looks varies differently from child to child. Some children may not be able to use and understand verbal communication, while others have more trouble understanding the subtle nuances of language, like tone of voice, and abstract ideas like puns or idioms. Of course, there are many children with autism who fall somewhere in between the two extremes.
2. **Restricted social interaction.** For a child on the more severe end of the spectrum, restriction in social interaction is very apparent. He may be seemingly uninterested in the people or events around him and very

inwardly focused. As you move from Level 3 to Level 1 support, this difficulty with social interaction is a little harder to define and discern. Some kids have difficulty following school rules because of the rigid and inflexible thinking patterns characteristic to autism, while others have difficulty making and maintaining friendships.

3. **Persistent patterns of (stereotypical) behavior.** Again, what this means varies from child to child, but it can include repetitive body movements known as "stimming"—hand flapping, rocking back and forth, or spinning. It can also include obsessive interests and trouble making adjustments to changes in routine.

Possible Educational Needs

The educational needs of a child with autism are as varied as the disorder itself. Depending on where your child's strengths and weaknesses lie, your child may simply need a little extra support around social skills and behavior in the regular education classroom. Or, he may need an entirely separate program that uses specific interventions to help him learn new skills, communicate (either verbally or by other means), increase his gross and fine motor skills, and/or help to address the unique sensory needs of a child with autism.

FACT

Many children with autism also have sensory issues and are very sensitive to sounds, lights, textures, smells, and other sensory stimuli that we take for granted. These stimuli can be overwhelming and can be the cause of seemingly unexplained meltdowns.

Deaf-Blindness

Deaf-blindness is an unusual category of disability that is used for children who have both visual and hearing impairments that together cause severe communication, developmental, and educational needs that can't be handled by either a program for children with just hearing impairments or a program for children with just visual impairments.

What Are the Characteristics of Deaf-Blindness?

In order to be found eligible under this category of disability your child must have both vision loss and hearing loss, but the degree of loss can vary. Your child doesn't need to be completely blind or deaf to be eligible for services. The key point is that it is the combined effect of the two disabilities that brings about your child's need for educational support.

Possible Educational Needs

The biggest challenges your child is going to face if she has deaf-blindness are communication and mobility. How is she going to be able to express herself so she can be understood, how is she going to understand other people well enough to learn, and how will she learn to navigate the school environment?

Most children who have this disabling condition will have already started some of this work in early intervention services before they even come to school, but a new environment will bring new challenges. Your child's program will need to be very individualized to make sure her unique limitations aren't getting in the way of learning. Not only will she need a way to learn about and understand the routine of her day, but she will also need a fairly predictable routine that she can rely on.

Deafness

In order to be eligible for special education under this category of disability, your child's hearing loss needs to be significant enough that he is limited in his ability to process "linguistic information through hearing, with or without amplification." More simply, that means that if your child isn't able to learn the information presented verbally in the regular education classroom even with a hearing aid or other device, he's eligible for special education services.

Possible Educational Needs

Your child's educational needs, as well as the type of staff and support that will be put in place are dependent on his current level of functioning. If your child uses sign language to communicate, an interpreter may be assigned to your child. Your child may also work with a speech-language pathologist to explore other ways of communicating, too, since the teachers and students around him may not know much sign language.

In his younger years, your child may benefit from a visual schedule, visual instructions, and other visual cueing in the regular education class-room. As he gets older, other accommodations, such as written notes for lectures and alternative modes of participation in group discussions and presentations, may be added to his program.

Emotional Disturbance

Emotional disturbance is difficult to consider as a parent, not only because of the impact of the difficulties your child faces in terms of mood and behav-ior, but also because emotional impairments aren't always as well under-stood as other disabilities. As a parent, you may worry about the implication of letting your child be "labeled" as having an emotional disturbance. How-ever, if your child is having trouble in school because of her impairment, it's important to keep in mind that the label is a way to access special education services as opposed to a definition of who your child is.

What Are the Characteristics of Emotional Disturbance?

Children with an emotional disturbance can have one of a number of diagnoses. In fact, some children with co-occurring conditions are found eligible for special education under this category because the way their dis-abilities affect their education fits more appropriately into the criteria for emotional disturbance than for another condition.

IDEA defines an emotional disturbance as a condition so pronounced that it makes it hard for a child to succeed in the regular education class-room. The condition also has to exhibit one or more of the following fea-tures over a long time period (IDEA, §300.8).

1. A failure to learn that isn't otherwise explained by intellectual, sensory, or health factors.
2. The lack of ability to create or sustain "satisfactory interpersonal rela-tionships with peers and teachers."

3. The exhibition of inappropriate feelings or behaviors under "normal circumstances."
4. A persistent unhappy or depressed mood.
5. An inclination to develop fears or physical symptoms around school and personal problems.

IDEA specifically includes schizophrenia in this category and specifically excludes children who are "socially maladjusted" and don't otherwise have an emotional disturbance. As one publication, *Social Maladjustment: A Guide to Differential Diagnosis and Educational Options*, explains it, socially maladjusted children "choose not to conform to socially acceptable rules and norms." This is different than children who are unable to do so because of mental health issues such as anxiety disorders, depression or bipolar disorder, obsessive-compulsive disorder, or other emotional disturbances.

Possible Educational Needs

The educational needs of a child with an emotional disturbance are incredibly dependent on the condition and what symptoms accompany it. Some children with emotional disturbances have a very difficult time regulating their emotions and behavior, and have violent, aggressive outbursts that put themselves or other children in the classroom at risk of harm.

If that's the case with your child, her special education program might be a smaller, more structured classroom with a teacher specifically trained in dealing with emotional disturbances and behavior issues. She may also benefit from social skills training groups and individual counseling. Other children might simply benefit from the support of a detailed behavior plan, an aide in the general education classroom, or even a modified school day if the symptoms of their disorder make it difficult to make it through an entire day of school.

Hearing Impairment

You might think it's strange that IDEA has different categories for deafness and hearing impairment, but even though the phrase "hearing impairment" can be used to describe deafness, IDEA has a separate definition for each of them. You'll remember that in order to be eligible for special education with deafness, your child's impairment needs to be so severe that he's not able to gain any of his information via sound. That's not the case with the hearing impairment category.

In this case, if your child has either a permanent or temporary hearing impairment that is adversely affecting his learning, then he can be found eligible for special education. The idea of a temporary hearing impairment may sound unusual, but it accounts for situations like kids who have frequent ear infections that make it hard for them to hear as well as other children. Regardless of whether the loss is permanent or temporary, the implication is that in this category of disability your child is able to respond to some type of auditory input, probably even speech.

Possible Educational Needs

If your child has some hearing loss or impairment, special education services aren't necessarily put into place to address issues with his intelligence. A child with a hearing impairment is more likely to have problems with speech and language development, which, in the long run, can cause some difficulties with reading and writing. That's because if your child isn't hearing like other children, he may not be picking up vocabulary, sentence structure, figures of speech, and other aspects of language that are tied to verbal communication.

Depending on how much your child is able to hear and produce speech, there are a number of different services and accommodations that can be put into place to support his general education. They include but aren't limited to:

- Speech and language services with a speech therapist
- Assistive technology
- Preferential seating in the classroom so that your child can hear better or read lips more efficiently
- Interpreter services for sign language
- Specially modified lessons, such as prepared lecture notes, captioned presentations, or even someone to take notes for your child

Intellectual Disability

Though the term *intellectual disability* has only been in use since 2010, the category of disability isn't new, simply renamed. It used to be called "mental retardation," a phrase that is still used to some extent. A child who has an intellectual disability has limited cognitive and adaptive functioning, meaning it's harder for him to complete both intellectual tasks and life skills. An intellectual disability is diagnosed by evaluating a child's IQ (or intellectual functioning) and his ability to perform everyday skills as compared to other children his age (adaptive functioning).

FACT

An average IQ score, as measured by one of the standardized intelligence tests given by a professional, is 100; a child is diagnosed as having an intellectual disability when his IQ is below 80.

What Are the Characteristics of an Intellectual Disability?

Intellectual disabilities can be mild, moderate, or severe, depending on a child's level of functioning. An intellectual disability isn't a disease, and there are a number of different causes and associated conditions. For instance, in certain genetic conditions, like Down syndrome, an intellectual disability is just one of many symptoms of the syndrome. An intellectual disability can also be caused by or the result of a number other things—too many to name—including oxygen deprivation, certain illnesses, and exposure to heavy metals like lead or mercury.

A child with an intellectual disability is able to learn but will do so at a slower pace than his peers. He may be slower to gain motor skills, have trouble remembering things he's learned, have difficulty understanding how to behave in socially appropriate ways, have a hard time with problem-solving and logical thinking, and have a hard time grasping the consequences of his own actions.

Possible Educational Needs

If your child has an intellectual disability, it's going to be very important to rely on the "individualized" component of an individualized education program. Though all children with intellectual disabilities should be able to participate in the general education classroom, for some it will be easier than others. If your child has a mild intellectual disability, he may need minimal support and modifications in the classroom as well as some time with a special education teacher for small-group or individual lessons.

The more severe the intellectual disability, the more specialized instruction your child will need. As your child approaches high school, you and his team will need to talk about what path is best for him in terms of transition. He may benefit greatly from participating in a vocational training or life skills program to help him be prepared for taking care of himself when he graduates or reaches age twenty-one.

Multiple Disabilities

This category is used when a child has more than one disability. In order to be found eligible for special education under multiple disabilities, the combination of the disabling conditions affects learning in a way that cannot be addressed by a program for just one of the disabilities. As an example, a child who has an intellectual disability and deafness has unique learning needs created by the combined impact of the two on her ability to function and learn.

Possible Educational Needs

Children with multiple disabilities can have significant trouble functioning and need a high level of educational and, often, medical support. What that support looks like differs depending on the combination of conditions, but many children will have limited communication skills, physical trouble getting around, and a hard time learning, using, and remembering skills.

Orthopedic Impairment

This category of disability covers a wide range of disabling conditions that cause a bodily impairment that affects your child's education. Among these conditions, IDEA includes impairments caused by *congenital anomaly or defect* (which are other names for congenital abnormalities, congenital malformation, or birth defects—something that is different about your child from the day he is born, such as a missing limb), orthopedic impairments caused by disease or injury, and those caused by other reasons.

What Are the Characteristics of Orthopedic Impairment?

The characteristics of orthopedic impairments depend on the cause, the body system the impairment impacts, and how severe the impairment is. Most orthopedic impairments fall in one of three main areas:

1. **Neuromotor impairments** that are a result of damage to the brain, nervous system, or spinal cord; they affect a person's ability to move one or more body parts. Two common neuromotor impairments are spina bifida and cerebral palsy. Since the systems that work together for motor skills and muscle coordination are affected, a child can have any number of limitations from bladder control problems to difficulty moving limbs to trouble with uncontrolled muscle movement.
2. **Degenerative diseases** like muscular dystrophy that affect motor development and often cause progressive loss of muscle tone.
3. **Musculoskeletal disorders** that are made up of any number of conditions that create physical limitations. Scoliosis, for example, is a musculoskeletal disorder, as is juvenile rheumatoid arthritis.

Possible Educational Needs

The educational needs of children with orthopedic impairments can't be narrowed down all that easily. Many children have no educational needs beyond the need to be able to physically access their learning, which can be helped both with classroom accommodations and related services to address motor needs. In cases where neuromotor involvement makes speech and writing difficult, assistive technology may also be part of your child's IEP.

Other Health Impairment

Children who qualify for special education under the category of other health impairment have one thing in common: They all have a chronic or an acute health problem that limits their "vitality, strength, and alertness" in a way that has a negative effect on their ability to learn without help.

What Are the Characteristics of an Other Health Impairment?

It's not as easy to sum up the most common features of this impairment, since it covers a wide variety of serious and chronic illnesses. IDEA provides a list of conditions that could be covered under this category but also makes it clear that just because your child's health condition isn't on the list doesn't mean your child can't qualify for services. The conditions the IDEA *does* mention are:

- Asthma
- ADD
- ADHD
- Diabetes
- Epilepsy
- Heart conditions
- Hemophilia
- Lead poisoning
- Leukemia
- Nephritis
- Rheumatic fever
- Sickle cell anemia
- Tourette's syndrome

There's a lot of overlap between the other health impairment category and conditions whose needs could be served by a 504 plan. When you and your child's team come to the table to discuss the results of evaluations and how she's doing in the classroom, if the accommodations she needs can be handled in the regular education classroom, she may end up with a 504 plan instead of being found eligible for special education.

Possible Educational Needs

The educational needs of children who are eligible for special education under Other Health Impairment can vary greatly depending on their specific condition. Many children may need what IDEA calls "school health services and school nurse services" to help with things like administering medication or managing medical equipment and care. Other children may need at-home or in-hospital tutoring because they're too medically fragile to attend school, while still others may need accommodations to the physical layout of their classroom. One thing that most children with OHI need in their plan is not for them at all—training and education for the school staff about the symptoms and implications of the health condition.

Specific Learning Disability

To qualify for special education under the specific learning disability category, obviously your child must have a learning disability. But even though the wording says "specific," the category doesn't only apply to limited types of learning disabilities. It does, however, say that learning problems that are the result of another type of disability covered in another category or arise from cultural, environmental, or economic differences should not be included in this category.

ESSENTIAL

IDEA recognizes that cultural, environmental, or economic disadvantages can have an effect on learning, but it's not always persistent and permanent, and not considered a special education need. To address this, IDEA 2004 put another program, known as Response to Intervention, into place to help kids who need extra support catch up to their peers.

What Are the Characteristics of Learning Disabilities?

Children who have learning disabilities have significant trouble in one area of learning, such as mathematical reasoning or calculations, writing, reading or reading comprehension, or in processing written or spoken language. This trouble has nothing to do with motivation or intelligence; it's caused by differences in how the brain processes the information. It's worth noting that if your child has a learning disability in one area, it doesn't mean he won't excel in another area. It's also worth noting that learning disabilities aren't all that uncommon. The National Center for Learning Disabilities estimates that one out of every five people has a learning disability.

Possible Educational Needs

The educational needs of children with learning disabilities can't be summarized because not only are there a number of different types of learning disabilities, but also some children may have severe learning disabilities while others only have mild learning disabilities. Still other children may have another impairment in addition to a learning disability, one that has its own sets of educational needs.

Regardless, IDEA 2004 says that during the process of evaluating whether your child has a learning disability, the school district should teach your child using a research-based intervention (one that has been proven to work the same way over time) and keep data to see how it works for your child. That response-to-intervention program's data can be used to help determine what types of educational program will be helpful (or not helpful) for your child.

Speech or Language Impairment

This category of disability applies to children who have a speech or language impairment that is usually part of a communication disorder. IDEA mentions, "stuttering, impaired articulation, a language impairment, or a voice impairment" as examples of characteristics of communication disorders that could impact your child's education (§300.8).

One thing to keep in mind about a speech or language impairment is that not being able to sound out certain letters, like *l*, *th*, or *w*, is within the normal range of development even when your child is in first and second grade. She may need a little help learning how to make those sounds, but that alone is not a communication disorder.

What Are the Characteristics of Speech or Language Impairments?

Speech and language impairments take a lot of different forms. Some are the cause of birth defects like a cleft palate, some are the result of damage to the speech-language center of the brain, some are due to a language-based learning disability, and some are just unexplained. Commonly a speech or language impairment will affect one or more of the following four areas:

1. **Articulation:** An articulation impairment is one that creates an inability to produce sounds correctly, such as lisping, substituting sounds for others, leaving out or adding sounds, or pronouncing sounds in a way that other people can't understand. As her parent, you may understand your child, but if most people can't, it's a good idea to have your child evaluated.
2. **Voice:** A voice impairment is one in which your child's voice has an abnormal quality in the way it sounds, whether it's due to the pitch, loudness, or other qualities. Your child may sound as though she always has a stuffed up noise, or sounds constantly hoarse.
3. **Fluency:** An impairment that affects fluency is one in which your child's normal speech flow is interrupted. This could be due to a stutter or stammer in which your child gets "stuck" on sounds, pieces of words, or entire words or in which she repeats or avoids those words and sounds. Fluency also refers to impairments in which your child's patterns of speech and breathing make her speech sound different than the more typical and expected patterns of a kid her age.
4. **Language:** A language impairment is one in which your child has trouble using language to express herself and/or has trouble understanding what other people are expressing.

Possible Educational Needs

Most children with a speech or language impairment will work with a speech-language therapist either one-to-one or in small groups to help improve their skills. As your child gets older, she may have problems with writing, language-intensive classwork, and social difficulties if she has trouble making herself understood. The speech-language therapist and special education teacher often work closely with regular education teachers to help them make appropriate accommodations in the classroom, including extra time for tests, alternatives to oral presentations, and, if necessary, the use of assistive communication devices.

Traumatic Brain Injury

To qualify for special education services under the category of traumatic brain injury (TBI), your child will have an "acquired injury to the brain" that causes trouble with thinking, problem-solving, language and information processing, memory and judgment, attention and reasoning, sensory-perceptual skills, physical functioning, and/or social functioning.

The key word here is "acquired." That means your child was not born with a brain injury or a disease that causes ongoing loss of brain functioning. An acquired brain injury is one caused by a physical force, such as an accident or a violent shaking.

What Are the Characteristics of Traumatic Brain Injury?

A TBI can drastically change a child's behavior and ability to learn. Depending on the extent of the injury and the course of recovery, a child with a TBI may have physical difficulties, including fatigue, headaches, trouble with muscle control, balance, vision, or basic motor skills. She may also experience trouble with memory, concentration, thinking quickly, or the planning of and understanding the sequence of a routine. Children with a TBI can also frequently have difficulty in regulating behavior and emotions.

Possible Educational Needs

The educational needs of a child with a traumatic brain injury are very specific to each individual and may change over time. Different types of brain injuries affect different skills. If motor skills are affected, physical therapy and occupational therapy services may be necessary to help a child find ways to navigate the physical aspects of learning. Some children will need one-to-one, specialized instruction because of memory or intellectual impairments, while others may require a behavior plan and assistive technology. The important thing to keep in mind is that an IEP is designed to meet those individual needs, so the team can assess what will be helpful for *your* child.

Visual Impairment

If you walk into a classroom full of kids, you're likely to see a number of kids wearing glasses to correct for a visual impairment, but those kids don't automatically qualify for special education services under this category. In order to be considered as having a visual impairment, your child's vision must impaired in such a way that even with correction it still has an adverse effect on his learning. Visual impairments include partial and complete blindness, but there are other conditions, too. For instance:

- **Congenital cataracts** are a condition in which the lens of the eye is cloudy, making it hard to see clearly.
- **Retinopathy of prematurity** is a condition that occurs in children who were born very early. In this condition the retina (the part of the eye sensitive to light) isn't completely developed.
- **Strabismus** (commonly known as "crossed eyes") is a condition in which a child's eyes do not focus on the same point at the same time.
- **Cortical visual impairment** is a brain disorder in which the brain isn't processing information from a child's eyes. It impairs vision even though it's not an eye-related condition.

What Are the Characteristics of Visual Impairment?

Children with visual impairments can miss out on a lot of learning, because a lot of learning is visual, including the ability to see and understand physical language cues. If your child has a visual impairment, he and his regular education teachers will need support around using his other senses to enhance his learning experience while making the most of and using tools to support the vision he does have.

Possible Educational Needs

An orientation and mobility specialist may be needed to help create a learning environment in which it is safe for your child to move around. That specialist can also teach your child ways to organize and negotiate the school independently.

CHAPTER 6

Do You Think Your Child Has a Learning Disability?

It's not unusual for kids to struggle with something in school once in a while; there's usually something that doesn't always come easily. For many children, a little extra practice or learning support can help fix the problem, but with other children that doesn't seem to work. If your child is constantly struggling in school and there's a pattern to the things he's having trouble with, you might be concerned that he has a learning disability. Learning disabilities aren't as uncommon as you might think, so if you're worried about it, it's a good idea to start gathering information about your concerns and talking to your child's teacher.

What Is a Learning Disability?

A learning disability has nothing to do with intelligence, nor does it have to do with your child needing to "try harder" or "live up to her potential." A learning disability is a disorder in which your child's brain doesn't interact with some of the information it receives in a typical or expected way. She's not able to process the information in the same way as her peers, making it harder—but not impossible—for her to learn certain skills. A learning disorder isn't always easy to spot, and it cannot be cured. However, once you know your child has a learning disability, she can be taught differently as well as given her own tricks and skills to make learning easier.

FACT

Learning disabilities tend to run in families, although the exact genetic link isn't yet clear. If you have a learning issue, your child has a higher than average risk of having one, too.

Here's Hallie's story:

When Hallie started kindergarten, she was eager to go to school and learn new things, but as the year progressed, Hallie became less willing to go to school. She was having more trouble than her peers in recognizing letters, letter sounds, and sight words, but when her parents and teacher talked it over they agreed a little extra practice at home might be helpful.

Night after night, Hallie and her parents practiced matching letters and sounds. Her parents read to her and tried to involve her in pointing out words she recognized, but Hallie wouldn't participate.

By the time Hallie got to first grade and the teacher started focusing on teaching kids to read, she was begging her mother to let her stay home from school. Getting her to read the required twenty minutes a day, do spelling homework, or complete word problems in math was almost impossible. Hallie's teacher started sending homework she didn't complete in class. Every time she was asked to identify a word or write a sentence, she would burst into tears, but she could recite all her math facts, was interested in science experiments, and excelled in other area of learning. Hallie's parents decided it was time to express their concerns.

Collecting Information about Your Concerns

You know your child is having trouble learning, but you don't know why. In order to talk to your child's teacher about your concerns, you're going to have to have more than a gut feeling that there's something wrong. It's a good idea to start writing down your concerns and observations over a period of time, using report cards, notes home, homework, and other paperwork as a way to support your worries. Using the information from Hallie's story, here's a sample of what that documentation might look like.

▼ CONCERNS ABOUT SCHOOL-RELATED ISSUES

Concerns	Supporting Evidence	Possible Related Factors	Interventions, Accommodations Tried/Suggested	Assessments Needed	Team Decisions
Unable to learn letters/ letter sounds and sight words.	Parental observation, teacher report, report cards, notes home	Fear of going to school	Extra practice at home		
Refusal (inability?) to read or write	Parental and teacher observation, work sent home	None known			

Notice that not all the information is filled out. That's because you can take the form with you to meetings and fill in the appropriate boxes as you and the school make decisions about your child's educational needs. A blank Concerns about School-Related Issues Chart can be found in Appendix C.

Bringing Your Concerns to the Teacher

Once you're able to name your concerns and have some documentation to back them up, set up an appointment with your child's teacher to talk. If you've already received phone calls or letters home about your child's performance, this can be a hard thing to do because it may feel like the teacher is blaming you, but for your child's sake, you need to set that aside. For the most part, teachers are genuinely concerned about their students and appreciate having good communication with parents.

What to Say to the Teacher

When you sit down with your child's teacher, it's a good idea to keep in mind this is mostly a time to gather and share information, not a time to guess at diagnoses. As you sit down, make it clear to the teacher that you're there to talk about your concerns about your child's learning, not to place blame.

ALERT

Always bring a pencil and a notebook or pad of paper when you meet with your child's teacher. You may not remember everything that's said, so you'll want to take notes to refer to later.

Take out your notes (or Concerns chart) and simply tell the teacher what you've observed and what you're worried about. Once you've had a chance to express that, ask your child's teacher some questions, too. Try asking open-ended questions, such as:

- What are you seeing in the classroom?
- Do you have any of the same concerns?
- What strategies have you found work well in the classroom?
- What has been tried that isn't working?
- Are there intervention programs in which my child can be included to see if it helps?
- Do you have any suggestions for how we can support her learning at home?
- What are your thoughts about referring for special education evaluation?

It's important that at this first meeting you don't have preconceived ideas of the answers you want to hear, because you might miss the chance to learn something you didn't already know about your child's classroom experience. Keep in mind, though, that if the teacher doesn't have any new suggestions or wants to take a "wait and see" approach, you don't have to agree. Nor do you need the teacher to initiate a referral for special education evaluation; that's something you can do yourself.

ALERT

Don't let your child's teacher tell you he's "too young" to diagnose with a learning disability. Children don't have to be a certain age before they can be diagnosed, and some learning issues can even diagnosed before children enter kindergarten.

Requesting Information about Making a Referral

Let's assume that you aren't satisfied with the answers you received and decide to initiate a referral for special education. You want to make sure you do it the right way. It's also important to make sure that your request for more information is part of your child's school record. That way if there's any question down the line about when the process was started, there's a paper trail. Using the story of Hallie as an example, here's a basic letter you can write to request more information about the process (a sample letter copy can be found in Appendix B).

October 1, 2014

To: School Principal, Teacher
Copy to: Hallie S.'s school record
Re: Requesting Information about Special Education Referral Process

I am writing to you in regard to my child, Hallie S., who is having difficulty in school. I have spoken with her teacher, Ms. X., in regard to my concerns. I know that there is a specific process to follow in order to initiate a referral for evaluation for special education services and would like to know more about how that process works. I am requesting that you please send me information about the process and how I can initiate a referral for evaluation.

Thank you for your assistance. I look forward to learning more about the special education referral process. Should you have any questions, I can be reached at the number below.

Respectfully,
Mr. and Mrs. S., Hallie's parents
Phone # 000-555-5555

Signs Your Child Might Have a Learning Disability

Though there aren't specific things that automatically indicate a learning disability, there are some signs that may point to the possibility that your child has one. Once you have had a chance to talk to your child's teacher, you probably have a lot more information about your child's strengths and weaknesses, information that you can combine with your own to look for some of these signs. The following checklists are not inclusive by any means, nor should you expect your child to show all of these signs, but it's a good place to start.

Signs of Reading Disabilities

Your child may need further evaluation for a learning disability in reading if he:

○ Has trouble remembering the names of the letters in the alphabet
○ Has difficulty making and remembering letter sounds
○ Doesn't easily recognize sight words and/or uses small sight words interchangeably when reading
○ Has trouble understanding how letters, sounds, and words are connected (i.e., doesn't get that each letter sound helps to make the whole word)

○ Has a limited vocabulary and has trouble understanding new vocabulary words

○ Has trouble sounding out and spelling words

○ Stops and starts and reads with hesitance

○ Comprehends things differently when reading versus being read to

Signs of Writing Disabilities

Your child may need further evaluation for a learning disability in writing if she:

○ Finds it hard to hold and use a pencil, pen, or crayon

○ Forms letters differently each time she writes them or consistently forgets how to write them

○ Finds it difficult to copy shapes and figures or draw lines

○ Is able to express herself with great detail verbally, but cannot do so in writing

○ Has messy, unevenly spaced handwriting

○ Has difficulty organizing her writing, either in outline form or when expressing her thoughts and ideas in writing

○ Finds proofreading and self-correction difficult

Signs of Math Disabilities

Math learning disabilities are varied, don't look the same in all children, and, depending on where her trouble lies, may show up at any time during your child's school career.

Your child may need further evaluation for a learning disability in math if she:

○ Has trouble sequencing numbers and other types of information

○ Finds noncomputational math concepts hard to grasp (i.e., calendar concepts, seasons)

○ Has difficulty recognizing and duplicating patterns, including simple object patterns and patterns in numbers. For example, your child may not be able to see the inverse relationship between addition and subtraction

○ Does not understand place value and has trouble with problems that require regrouping
○ Finds it difficult to follow the order of operations in a math problem
○ Doesn't line the numerals up correctly when writing a problem
○ Has difficulty understanding fractions, percentages, and geometry
○ Finds it hard to count money and make change
○ Has trouble estimating costs and/or keeping a budget
○ Has trouble estimating time or keeping to a time-related schedule

ESSENTIAL

Believe it or not, clumsiness can be tied to math learning disabilities. Children who have trouble with visual-spatial math can also have trouble judging distances between objects and have a poor sense of direction. This can make some physical activities, like running or catching a ball, hard to manage.

Signs of Language Disabilities

There are many different kinds of language disorders, some of which are learning disabilities and some of which are communication disorders. The signs on this checklist combine signs of all these different types of disorders, so not all signs will be applicable to all children with this type of learning disability. You may want to explore further evaluation if your child:

○ Has trouble understanding the meaning of what people say when they speak
○ Voices her thoughts slowly and gets frustrated when she can't find words to explain herself
○ Can describe or make a picture of something but can't find the right word for it
○ Has difficulty giving names of objects
○ Finds jokes, idioms, puns, and other metaphorical language confusing
○ Says words that sound similar incorrectly or substitutes them for each other

○ Leaves out syllables or parts of sentences in speech or writing
○ Has trouble following multistep, verbal directions
○ Finds it difficult to follow a conversation when many people are speaking and/or people are talking fast
○ Asks "What?" a lot even though she's heard you
○ Is easily distracted by background noises
○ Has trouble understanding nonverbal cues

Signs of Visual-Perceptual Disabilities

A child who has visual-perception learning disabilities isn't having trouble seeing—her brain isn't processing the visual information correctly. Your child may have such a disability if she:

○ Finds it hard to get from one place to another, even in her own neighborhood
○ Has difficulty keeping her place in a book
○ Reverses or inverts similar-looking letters. For example, writes or mistakes *w* for *m* or *p* for *q*
○ Moves the paper instead of the scissors when she's cutting
○ Moves her head to follow the text when reading a book
○ Doesn't recognize an object or a familiar word if she only sees a part of it

Types of Learning Disabilities

As you can see, the phrase "learning disability" can apply to any number of types of neurological disorders that affect your child's ability to receive, sort through, store, recall, and express information. There are some specific types of learning disabilities that are more common than others. Although the diagnosis can provide some information about what your child may have trouble learning, it does not identify your child's specific trouble in that area of learning.

Type of Learning Disability	Problematic Areas	May Cause Problems With
Dyscalculia	Math	Number sense, memorization, number recognition
Dysgraphia	Writing, written expression	Handwriting, spelling, grammar and syntax, organization written ideas
Dyspraxia	Fine motor skills	Completing motor tasks, dexterity, speech, coordination
Dyslexia	Reading, spelling, writing	Fact recall, rules of spelling/grammar, understanding directions, spatial orientation, reading
Nonverbal Learning Disability	Visual-spatial, social skills, organization and planning	Social relationships, spatial awareness (clumsiness), conversational skills, cognitive flexibility

ADHD Is Not a Learning Disability

You may have noticed that ADHD (attention deficit hyperactivity disorder) is not mentioned on the list of learning disabilities. That's because while ADHD can affect learning, it's not a learning disability. It shares some of the same features as a learning disability, and, according to the National Center for Learning Disabilities, is a co-occurring condition in one-third of children who have been diagnosed with a learning disability, but it in itself is not one.

What Is ADHD?

ADHD is a brain-based disorder, meaning that something in the brain or neurological functioning is causing the symptoms, as opposed to it being a purely behavioral issue. If your child has ADHD, he may have trouble concentrating, focusing, organizing himself and his surroundings, following directions well, and controlling his activity level and impulses. Many children's symptoms are well managed with a combination of medication and behavioral therapy.

Types of ADHD

To make things even more difficult to figure out, there are two main types of ADHD, the symptoms of which can look very different from each other. Both types can cause symptoms that are easily confused with some learning disabilities, which is one of the reasons it's so important to make sure your child has a thorough evaluation before he is diagnosed with any of these conditions. The two types of ADHD are inattentive (sometimes known simply as ADD) and hyperactive-impulsive.

Inattentive Type ADHD

If your child has this type of ADHD, he may have trouble keeping focused and staying organized, both of which can have a negative impact on his ability to learn. He may:

- Seem as though he's daydreaming a lot of the time
- Not appear to listen to you or pay attention to details
- Process information slowly and have difficulty following directions
- Have a hard time keeping his attention on something for a sustained period of time
- Lose things, appear disorganized, and get bored quickly.

ESSENTIAL

There is also a third type of ADHD, known as Combined Type. Children with this type show all the key symptoms of ADHD: inattention, overactivity, impulsivity, and distractibility.

Hyperactive-Impulsive Type ADHD

This type of ADHD is the more commonly known type of the disorder. If your child has hyperactive-impulsive ADHD, he may:

- Be in constant motion and fidgety
- Have difficulty staying in one place or sitting still
- Talk constantly

- Act impulsively without thinking about what's going to happen
- Have uncontrollable outbursts of emotion or temper
- Have trouble maintaining friendships and taking turns, and interrupt frequently

How ADHD Can Affect Learning

As you can imagine, all types of ADHD have the potential to impact your child's ability to learn. The symptoms of ADHD can get in the way of your child's academic success in a variety of different ways, regardless of what type of the disorder he has. Whether your child has trouble organizing himself, can't pay attention long enough to complete homework, or is unable to stay still long enough to benefit from the teacher's instructions, his education can suffer. If your child has poor impulse control, his frustration over not being able to focus can lead to outbursts that disrupt the classroom (and learning) and impact his relationship with his peers.

On top of that, poor impulse control, trouble paying attention to details, and processing information slowly can make it very difficult for your child to learn and follow through with problem-solving skills. This can have an effect not only on social skills but also in all areas of learning that require your child to use more abstract and analytical thinking skills.

How to Get Special Education Services for Your Child with ADHD

Just because ADHD isn't a learning disability doesn't mean your child won't qualify for special education services. Many children who have ADHD qualify under the other health impairment (OHI) category because they have a condition that causes, in IDEA's words, impairment in "alertness, including a heightened alertness to environmental stimuli." IDEA also says that if this heightened alertness causes your child to be less alert to the educational environment, that can be affecting her education.

Each state has different policies about how kids with ADHD can be found eligible for special education services under OHI. In Connecticut, for example, the state has added ADHD as a subcategory to OHI, making it much easier for you to get an IEP in place for your child. In Florida, on the other hand, your child must undergo extensive educational testing to rule out any other contributing factors, have a 504 plan in place that hasn't met her educational needs, *and* have a medical diagnosis of ADHD before she can be found eligible.

Section 504 versus Other Health Impairment

If your child is found ineligible for an IEP and is having trouble being successful in the regular education classroom, she can still get accommodations put into place under a 504 plan. If you remember, the goal of Section 504 is to make sure people with disabilities have equal access to free appropriate education.

If your child doesn't have any learning deficits that need to be addressed by a special education program, then getting an appropriate education is a matter of making some modifications to the general education classroom to help reduce the impact her ADHD symptoms have on her learning.

Common Accommodations for ADHD

Accommodations are individualized, depending on your child's needs, but there are some that are more commonly used for kids with ADHD. They include:

- Preferential seating near the front of the classroom and away from distractions
- Providing extra time to complete work or giving shorter assignments
- Giving both oral and written directions
- Providing written lecture notes or having a designated note taker
- Building in time to check work before handing it in
- Using a behavior chart or plan to encourage appropriate interactions and classroom behaviors
- Allowing for short breaks as needed

CHAPTER 7

More about Section 504

There's nothing more frustrating than watching your child struggle in school only to be told he's not having enough trouble to qualify for special education. While IDEA's detailed rules and regulations around eligibility have made schools more responsible for providing special education for kids with disabilities, sometimes they are so rigid that some children who have disabilities are not found eligible for special education. If that happens with your child, instead of giving up, it's time to reconvene and talk about putting a 504 plan in place.

Why Bother with a 504 Plan?

When your child is found ineligible for special education services, the school isn't saying that your child doesn't have a disability, or that he doesn't need modifications in school to make it easier for the effects of that disability. What they are saying is that all the information about your child—evaluations, observations, report cards, grades—don't show that his disability is making learning so difficult that he's not able to learn in the regular education classroom without specific specialized instruction.

However, what isn't being said is just as important as what is being said. Your child may not need specialized instruction to learn in the regular education classroom, but is his disability severely limiting him in some way that's making it hard for him to get the same benefit in the classroom as his peers? That's the question you need to ask yourself and his teachers before you decide not to bother with a 504 plan.

An Example: Sally's Story

When Sally was a preschooler it was discovered she had a severe peanut allergy. Even the slightest contact with peanuts or tree nut products could be life threatening. When she entered public school, the school administrators saw this information and told her parents that Sally qualified for a 504 plan to make accommodations for her allergy. Sally's parents declined, noting that Sally had no trouble learning and they didn't want her to feel any more singled out than she already did. They said they would leave an EpiPen with the nurse in case of emergencies and leave it at that.

During the first month of school, Sally came home and complained to her parents that she had to sit away from her friends at snack time and lunch; she wasn't allowed to eat any of the snacks friends brought in for special treats, and she couldn't use the same water fountains as the other kids. When Sally's parents sat down with the school to talk about their concerns, they were told the measures were put in place for Sally's protection.

In Sally's case, her peanut allergy is a disabling condition that isn't affecting her ability to learn, but it does have an effect on whether or not she gets to participate in her education like her peers. In this situation it would have been worth it to bother with a 504 plan. Her 504 plan would address the issues that set her apart from the other kids and impact her major life activities.

As a kindergartener, Sally is really too young to take on the responsibilities of the specialized self-care her disability requires. She's not able to read labels to see what the ingredients of a special snack are, she's not able to tell whether her friends have peanut-based products for lunch, and she's unable to make sure that her table area is completely clean and safe for her.

Because her allergy is life threatening, it's not unlikely that one of the accommodations addressed in her 504 plan would be making the entire school peanut-free or, at the very least, her classroom. Her 504 plan would ensure that information is sent home to all the parents about why the campus is peanut-free, make it clear where her EpiPen will be stored, and make sure that all school personnel are trained to recognize the signs and symptoms of an allergic reaction.

Getting Services under Section 504

Not all children with allergies would qualify for service under Section 504. Sally's case and those of other kids like her are different because the allergy severely limits their activities. A child whose allergies cause a runny nose, a rash, or other milder symptoms doesn't need any special accommodations to be like other kids in the classroom. To qualify for a 504 plan, your child must have a significant physical or mental impairment that is chronic or expected to last a long period of time. That impairment must somehow get in the way of her ability to participate in a major life activity.

FACT

Section 504 says a child can qualify if life activities are affected because of other people's reaction to her impairment. For instance, a child who has severe scars that don't affect her but cause her peers to treat her as if she were impaired can qualify for a 504 plan.

The steps for getting a 504 plan in place aren't all that different than getting an IEP put into place—you still have to request a meeting and have documentation of your child's disability and difficulty in school. If you think your child should have a 504 plan, start by mentioning to your child's teacher that you are going to request a meeting. Then, write a letter to the principal requesting that meeting. It's important to put your request in writing so that there is a paper trail of your attempts to get some help for your child. You can find a sample letter in Appendix B but here's what a letter from Sally's parents to the principal might look like.

Dear Mr. Principal,

We are writing to formally request a meeting to create a 504 plan for our daughter, Sally. As you know, she has a life-threatening peanut allergy, a condition that impacts her daily functioning in school.

Enclosed you will find documentation of her condition from her doctor, including information about how the allergy manifests and its severity. We will also bring a copy of this documentation to the meeting with us. Please let us know if you require any further information prior to meeting.

We have spoken with Sally's teacher about our intent to request this meeting. In order to make sure a plan can be developed and appropriate accommodations implemented in a timely manner, we would like to have this meeting as soon as possible.

Please let us know of the soonest meeting times and dates at which all of the necessary school personnel can attend. In Sally's case, we feel it's crucial to have the school nurse involved in this meeting.

We look forward to hearing from you within the next week about the request for a meeting.

Thank you for your help.

Sincerely,
Mr. and Mrs. Y. (Sally's parents)

Enclosure: physician's statement

As you can see, just like with IDEA, deciding whether your child is eligible for a 504 plan is a team decision, but the eligibility requirements are different.

The Benefits of a 504 Plan

The major benefit of having a 504 plan in place is to have a record of the accommodations being made for your child. Many experienced teachers will put informal modifications in place, and sometimes a school will provide some extra support in the classroom if they can. While that's all helpful to your child, if your child is going to need these accommodations on a continuing basis, then the accommodations need not only to be legally documented but also agreed upon by the entire team. Without the legal document in place, no one is required to continue making modifications for your child.

With a 504 plan in place, the accommodations become formalized and a part of your child's record. This is helpful in two ways: It's something you can turn to later on if your child is still struggling and you want to pursue special education evaluation, and if your child switches schools for any reason, there is already a plan that the new school can follow or use as a guide.

What a 504 Plan Includes

Not all school districts use the same format or template for a 504 plan, but the basic information it includes is the same. At the very least, your child's 504 plan will include:

- His name and identifying information (date of birth, address, parents' names, grade, teacher, school he attends, etc.)
- The date the plan was written and how long it will be in place
- A section to describe his areas of strengths and a section to describe the areas of concern
- Specific accommodations to address each area of concern, what personnel in the school is responsible for implementing each accommodation, and on what date the accommodation will begin
- A place for all meeting participants to sign to indicate agreement with the plan

In addition to the basic information, many schools will also attach a copy of any documentation they have of your child's disability as well as any behavior plan that has been put into place.

ALERT

Unlike under IDEA, Section 504 doesn't include parents as part of the decision-making team. Each school district can make its own policies as to how involved parents get to be in the development of a 504 plan. However, your child cannot have a 504 plan without you knowing about it.

How a 504 Plan Is Different from an IEP

The main difference between a 504 plan and an IEP is the laws that they are tied to. A 504 plan is tied to a civil rights law, so it gives your child with a disability protection from discrimination in getting equal access to an appropriate education. An IEP is tied to a detailed special education law, so it provides protections and services for your child only if she is eligible for special education. Another difference is that accommodations in a 504 plan are implemented in the regular education classroom, while an IEP provides special education services. But those aren't the only difference between the two.

ESSENTIAL

Unlike with IDEA, a school district is not required to evaluate a child under Section 504 upon parent request. If the school doesn't think a child needs services due to a disability, they have the right to refuse to refer for evaluation.

IDEA has very strict requirements about what information needs to be contained in a written plan (the IEP) and the language that has to be used to write it. Technically, a 504 plan doesn't even have to be a written plan of action; it just has to be a documented plan. That means your child's 504 plan could actually just be a written summary of what was discussed and agreed upon at the 504 meeting.

FACT

A child with a 504 plan will be in the regular education classroom unless he "is so disruptive in a regular classroom that the education of other students is significantly impaired" and the child's needs can't be addressed in the regular classroom. (34 C.F.R. §104.34, Appendix A, #24)

Both plans, however, provide your child with rights and protections when it comes to her education. If an IEP isn't an option, it's worth taking the time to see if your child qualifies for a 504 plan, even if you're not as pleased with the amount of detail.

Some Conditions That Qualify for a 504 Plan

Although the accommodations in your child's 504 plan are tailored to his specific strengths and weaknesses based on his disability, there are some disabling conditions that, because they present similarly in many kids, have some frequently used modifications.

Suggested 504 Accommodations for ADHD

If your child has ADHD and isn't found eligible for special education under the other health impairment category, then he's likely to qualify for a 504 plan because the symptoms can affect the major life activity of learning (and maybe social skills, too). Some typical accommodations for ADHD include:

- Preferential seating closer to the teacher and farther away from distractions, such as windows, doors, or other busy areas
- Providing a written copy or audio recording of lecture notes and verbal instructions
- Allowing extra time to complete written assignments and tests

- Allowing for note sharing so that difficulty with handwriting doesn't get in the way of learning
- Providing frequent movement breaks, access to a large therapy ball instead of a chair, and/or allowing a student to work standing up
- Establishing a system of nonverbal cues with teachers to help your child know when he's losing focus or behaving inappropriately, as well as providing positive reinforcement for appropriate behavior
- Giving five-minute warnings before activity changes and transitions
- Posting visual rules and schedules
- Providing extra assistance in organization of time and materials

Suggested 504 Accommodations for Asthma

Not all children who have asthma have severe enough symptoms that it will affect them in school. However, if your child might need to take his inhaler while at school, or his asthma is not well controlled, then creating a 504 plan is a good idea. Some of the accommodations that can be put into place include:

- Training the school staff who work with your child in monitoring for signs and symptoms of an asthma attack
- Developing a plan for who will dispense medication and who will be a backup in case that person isn't available, as well as training those people in how inhalant therapies work
- Creating an emergency plan in the case that your child's medication doesn't help his breathing
- Allowing for time to rest as necessary and make a plan about how your child will participate at recess and in physical education classes
- Creating a "scent-free" school and getting that information out to all parents and students

Suggested 504 Accommodations for Diabetes

If your child has diabetes, if he doesn't have an IEP, then he definitely needs to have a 504 plan. It's crucial to make sure that all the staff in the school are aware of your child's condition and have some training about what diabetes is and what a diabetic crisis looks like. Beyond that, though, your child's 504 plan will have some very specific accommodations about daily routines and dealing with crises. These may include:

- For younger children, making sure there is staff and backup staff trained in checking blood sugar levels and to administer insulin, if necessary
- For older children (high school age), making sure there is a place your child can go to check blood sugar levels and administer medication, as well as making sure there is a staff member who can oversee the process
- Making sure that all school personnel are trained to recognize the symptoms of unstable blood sugar levels and how to respond—this includes not only in-school personnel but bus drivers and afterschool activity directors, too
- Providing time and space for your child to eat when he needs to in order to keep his blood sugar level stable—this may mean your child's lunch period is changed to a different time and/or that he is given extra time for lunch and snack

As you can see, the accommodations that can be put into place for your child are flexible and geared toward his specific needs. This should be true whether he has a 504 plan or an IEP.

CHAPTER 8

Trying Something Else First: Response to Intervention

One of the results of IDEA 2004 and NCLB aligning a little more closely to make sure that all students—not just children who are eligible for special education—have the support they need to be successful in school is that schools were encouraged to put into place programs known as Response to Intervention (or RTI). Response to Intervention allows schools the flexibility to use research-based interventions to meet the needs of children who are struggling with learning or behavior in the classroom but who may not need a referral for special education.

What Is RTI?

RTI is less of a specific program and more of a flexible process that uses testing to look at how your child and his peers are doing in various areas of learning (for instance, writing, addition, multiplication, reading comprehension, etc.). Because it's a flexible process, if an entire classroom in a school isn't at the expected academic level in one area, a classroom-wide intervention might be put into place to help the whole class. If there's a small group of students who still need help after that, then small-group instruction will be put into place. If after a period of small-group instruction your child still needs some extra help, individual help can be provided.

ESSENTIAL

Just because your child is in a response-to-intervention program doesn't mean he can't be evaluated for special education. In fact, if your child has a suspected learning disability, trying RTI during the evaluation period provides good information about what type of intervention might be helpful for your child.

The "intervention" in RTI is the key in understanding what the program is all about: intervening before your child (or a group of children) falls too far behind peers. RTI is a proactive program, meaning that your child can be identified as needing a little help earlier than he would be when it comes to special education referral. One of the goals of RTI is to reduce the number of children who are referred for special education by getting a good sense of the students who will be able to move forward after a stretch of intensive extra help, and by recognizing those who will need ongoing learning support.

The really good news is that intervention programs usually take place in the regular education classroom and there are increasing levels of intervention, so if the first thing the school tries doesn't work, there are other options before moving on to special education evaluation or simply moving on.

Research-Based Interventions

Don't think that your child's teacher is just guessing at ways to try to help; the key piece of RTI is that schools must use *research-based interventions* and keep data tracking your child's progress. A research-based intervention is a program or way of teaching that has been proven to work to improve skills and academic performance. Many school districts have a curriculum coordinator who keeps track of what programs are being used successfully as interventions in the different subject areas. If you have questions about the types of intervention programs your school uses, get in touch with your child's principal. If he doesn't have that information, he should be able to tell you who does.

QUESTION

Are Response to Intervention programs only for reading and writing?
Though the majority of RTI research and interventions deal with literacy learning, RTI is about addressing trouble areas to improve learning. The tier-based model of teaching skills can also be applied to teaching math.

It's important to know that RTI instruction is a fluid process, so there's no deadline by which your child has to be signed up to be included in the intervention. If at any time during the school year you have concerns, you can talk to your child's teacher or the school principal and ask about what interventions are available to assist your child. The whole idea of RTI is to take kids where they're at skill-wise and help them gain skills to get to grade-level expectations. That means adjustments to how your child is being taught are made based on *his* response to an intervention, not the response of all the students in his class or a small group.

ESSENTIAL

If your child is in an RTI program, you should get a written intervention plan. The plan should describe the intervention, how long the intervention will last, who is involved in your child's intervention, and how progress will be measured and reported.

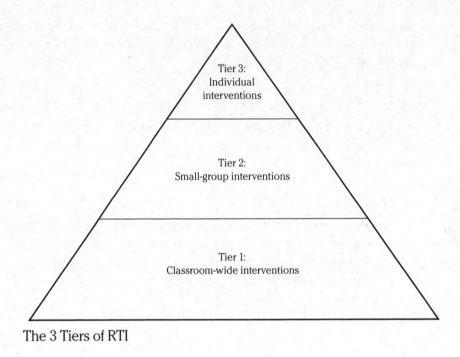

The 3 Tiers of RTI

The Basics of How RTI Works

The RTI process typically has three levels. The first level, Tier 1, is put into place when your child's entire classroom isn't where they need to be in a specific area of learning. That's usually determined by the results of school-wide standardized testing and your state's expectations for the grade level. After a period of time, usually one to two months, of using a research-based intervention to teach the entire class, your child's teacher will re-examine the skills of the class to see whether the intervention is helping.

If most kids are making good academic progress, the teacher will then identify the children who are still struggling, and those kids might move to the second level, Tier 2, for some small-group instruction. Your child's baseline, or starting, skills will be tested and documented, as will her progress over the course of the small-group instruction. After a period of time—how much time varies with the school and the intervention program—your child's teacher will use the same testing to see where your child's skills are now and either graduate her from the small group or move her to the third level, Tier 3, for more intensive individual instruction.

FACT

Tier 3 individual instruction isn't necessarily special education. Although a referral for special education services may be a possibility, the goal of RTI is to provide interventions to make sure your child has a good chance to improve her skills in the general education environment.

The Three Tiers of RTI

Being able to see RTI as a pyramid gives you a very good representation of how the process narrows its focus to provide higher levels of intervention to the smaller number of kids who need it. It works exactly like it looks; at each level or tier, the number of kids who need more intervention is less. At each level, the intervention program is more individualized.

Tier 1: Classroom-Wide Interventions

If your child's class is participating in the first level of a response-to-intervention program, what happens in the classroom won't be all that much different than it was before. Your child's teacher will essentially take a new approach to teaching the skills. Your child and her classmates will participate in a screening or pretest. That gives the teacher a chance to see where their skills are before she tries a new way of teaching or, in the case of behavioral concerns, interacting with the students. The Response to Intervention Action Network estimates between 80 and 90 percent of students will show improvement after participating in Tier 1 interventions.

Tier 2: Small-Group Interventions

If you assume your child's classroom has thirty students in it, then that means that at least twenty-four of them will be meeting the grade-level expectations after the first level of intervention. That leaves a fairly small number of kids (six) who may need intervention in a small group. That's the narrowing of the pyramid.

A Tier 2 intervention is in addition to your child's classroom instruction, not instead of it. Your child is likely to participate in a small-group activity or lesson two to three times a week for at least ten weeks. You may also be asked to work with her at home. During that time, data is collected on your child's progress so at the end of the session it's clear whether or not the small-group instruction has been helping. Nearly 95 percent of the students in Tier 2 will improve academically.

Tier 3: Individual Interventions

Mathematically, if 95 percent of those six kids in Tier 2 respond to the second level of intervention, then there's not even a whole kid left who didn't improve. However, since we're talking about real kids, not just numbers, it's possible that your child will still be struggling in school after intensive small-group instruction. At that point, it's time to do two things: It's time to start the referral for a special education evaluation process (if you haven't already), and it's time to talk to the school about what individualized interventions and support can be put into place while that process is in motion.

The Benefits of RTI

You might be wondering why to even bother with Response to Intervention if your child is going to end up being referred for special education anyway. There are benefits to Response to Intervention. Firstly, it's important to keep in mind that the majority of children don't end up being referred for special education after participating in solid, research-based interventions.

Secondly, even if your child does need to be evaluated for special education, the school district has up to forty-five school days after you sign the parental consent form before the initial eligibility meeting has to be held. Counting weekends and school vacations, depending on when the referral is made, that can be almost as long as three months. With RTI in place in the meantime, you're not taking a "wait and see" approach to his learning; your child is getting some extra help in the academic areas in which he is struggling. Not to mention, all of his progress in RTI is being documented. That documentation can become a part of the process of determining eligibility for special education, especially since it provides information about what type of instruction is and is not helping your child.

Being an Advocate in Your Child's RTI Experience

It may seem as though Response to Intervention is just another in-school program, but being an active part of the intervention process and advocating for your child isn't just your right; it can also really help your child, too. Dr. Rachel Brown-Chidsey, PhD, NCSP, coauthor of the book *Response to Intervention: Principles and Strategies for Effective Practice*, thinks the more supportive of RTI parents are and the more questions they ask, the more they help to make schools create better response-to-intervention programs.

Dr. Brown-Chidsey says parents should be asking teachers and administrators what instructional services are offered at each tier level and how parents are informed about the instruction and its results. Other ways you can advocate for your child when it comes to Response to Intervention include:

- Ask about the response-to-intervention programs your school district provides at each grade level and for what subject areas. Your school district should have an RTI plan in place. If it doesn't, start asking why and when it will be putting a plan in place.
- Find out what specific interventions are being used. Remember, the interventions have to be research based, and your child's teacher needs a way to be able to track progress. An intervention program is not the same as making modifications in the classroom to seating arrangements or workload.
- Don't accept "It costs too much" as an answer. Two of the most widely used programs for Response to Intervention, the Dynamic Indicators of Basic Early Literacy Skills (DIBELS) and AIMSweb (AIMS stands for Academic Improvement Measurement System), are either free or very low-cost programs for school districts.
- Be a little bit patient. It can be hard to stand back and watch while your child is struggling in school, but interventions don't work overnight. To get a good idea of whether or not an intervention is helping with enough data to prove it, the strategy has to be used for a minimum number of weeks (usually four) before something else is tried.
- Say something if you think your child isn't getting any benefit. Response to Intervention is a "try something else first" approach, not

a "try this and nothing else" approach to helping students. You have the right at any time to request your child be evaluated for special education if you think that's what she needs to help her learn.

Ten RTI Resources for Parents

Being an active participant in the Response to Intervention process relies not only on you knowing about your child's specific program, but also on your ability to judge whether it's appropriately addressing your child's needs. Here are some resources to learn more about RTI and how you can be a part of the process.

1. **International Reading Association:** With a specific focus on literacy interventions, the International Reading Association website has a number of resources about Response to Intervention, including podcasts, downloadable booklets and brochures, and basic articles.

2. **Intervention Central:** This website, created by RTI consultant Jim Wright, provides a number of forms and manuals, as well as lists and explanations of research-based interventions that your child's school might try.

3. **National Association of School Psychologists fact sheet,** *Response to Intervention (RTI): A Primer for Parents*: This easy-to-read, downloadable fact sheet is just one of the many articles the National Association of School Psychologists has available to help parents better understand the RTI process.

4. **Response to Intervention: Information for Families:** This informational website is a project of PAVE (Partnerships for Action Voices for Empowerment) and aims to inform parents about the RTI process and at-home activities that can be used to support their children's learning.

5. **The ABCs of RTI in Elementary School: A Guide for Parents:** This twenty-eight-page booklet is a parent primer of elementary school interventions. It has a wealth of information about various types of interventions, how the process works, and how parents and schools can start working together.

6. **The ABCs of RTI in Middle School: A Guide for Parents:** This twenty-six-page booklet provides a look at how RTI is applicable in middle school. It uses real-life examples of situations in which RTI can be helpful, and

provides parents with a framework of information that can help them ask questions and make decisions for their child.

7. **The National Center on Response to Intervention:** rti4success, as this center is known, is the go-to resource to find anything you want to know about RTI. From a resource library to information about interventions to a live chat function, the website can help walk you through the entire RTI process.

8. **The National Center on Learning Disabilities' Parent's Guide to Response to Intervention:** This all-inclusive guide to RTI not only provides the basics of the system and how it works, but it also defines common RTI terms that can be helpful to know in keeping the lines of parent-school communication open.

9. **National Research Center on Learning Disabilities:** In addition to basic information about RTI, the NRCLD provides parental information about how RTI can be used to help in identification of learning disabilities. You can also download a parent primer—*ABCs of RTI*.

10. **The Response to Intervention Action Network:** This comprehensive website not only provides basic information, checklists, and other resources for parents, but it also hosts discussion boards where parents can connect with each other.

CHAPTER 9

Keeping Involved in Your Child's Education

Until your child starts school, be it preschool or public school, for most of his life he's had one teacher day in and day out—you. Parents often underestimate the role they play as being the first and most important teacher in their child's life. That's why early intervention services most often take place in the home. When your child goes to school, you're no longer the only one who is in charge of what he learns, but it doesn't mean that you're not part of his education, or that you're no longer one of his teachers. Being actively involved in your child's education is crucial to helping your child be successful in school. Keeping track of your child's progress and forging a good parent-school relationship will serve you well when it comes to advocating for your child's special education needs. Keeping involved in your child's education takes a lot of concerted effort on your part, but once you have some sort of system in place, it's fairly easy to maintain.

Getting to Know the School

If your child's school is new to you, or if you haven't gotten to know it well, it can only help you to get to know a little more about the school itself before talking with anyone about special education services or an evaluation for your child. That way, when you go into meetings, you can really focus on your child's needs and not get hung up on basic school rules and regulations you didn't already know.

Each school district, and sometimes schools within a district, has different codes of conduct, hours, rules about visitors, and other unique ways of handling situations. Read through the school handbook (or ask for a copy if you don't have one) to learn all about the school and its policies, so you can see if any of them have a direct effect on your child's ability to learn.

ALERT

Some schools have a zero tolerance policy, in which there's little room for children to make mistakes without punishment. If your child's disability affects his behavior, talk to the individualized education program (IEP) team about how this policy will be handled in your child's case.

Getting to Know Your Child's Teacher

One of the best ways to stay involved with your child's education is to taking time to get to know her teacher. Since her teacher spends the entire day with her, sees her in a learning environment, and gets to see how she interacts with her peers, her teacher may be the person who gets to know your child almost as well as you. Starting out with a good line of communication makes it easier when you're advocating for your child's need for special education.

Attending open houses and classroom events when you can shows that you're interested in the whole learning process, not just what the teacher can do for your child. And establishing a good relationship with your child's teacher makes it easier to have a more in-depth conversation about your concerns and, hopefully, gain an ally who will help you advocate for your child.

What to Do about an Unfair Teacher

Unfortunately, there will also be times when, despite your best efforts, you can't open a line of communication. Maybe the teacher is unwilling to engage with you, or you just don't like her attitude. There are some teachers who are easily frustrated by the challenges of children who have trouble learning or are disruptive in the classroom, even if there's a disability behind those troubles. Sometimes that frustration can be aimed at your child and, peripherally, you. But, unless your child is already in the middle of your dispute, it's better to leave her out of it. If she's already having trouble in school, adding stress and tension to that isn't a great idea.

That doesn't mean you shouldn't address your concerns about your child's teacher. In fact, if you feel as though the teacher is singling out your child, there are steps you can take to address it that are separate from the special education process. You can think of it as the four Ds of dealing with a difficult teacher:

- **Detecting.** This is an information-gathering phase. Your child has probably told you about things going on in the classroom that are upsetting to her or that she feels as though she's being treated unfairly. Ask your child for specific, detailed examples of what's happening. If you feel comfortable doing so, it's a very good idea to ask your child's teacher about the incidents she describes, using words like "I'd like to understand what happened; can you give me your perspective of this incident?"
- **Documentation.** This isn't just a one-time thing, it's an ongoing process. Keep a communication log of phone conversations and at-the-classroom door encounters (see the Parent Communication Log later in this chapter for an example). Print out any e-mails you send the teacher or the teacher sends you. Keep notes at home, and make copies of any notes you send in.
- **Discussion.** Once you think you have an idea of what's happening, set up a meeting with the teacher and the principal to talk about your concerns with the teacher or how your child is being treated in the classroom. Keep calm and stick to the facts. The more accusatory you appear, the less likely you are to be taken seriously. If you don't get satisfactory results or feel like you've been heard, keep scheduling

meetings, but with different people. For example, talk to the superintendent of schools or the school board if necessary.

- **Dissention.** You've already made yourself clear verbally, and if nothing has changed, it's time to step it up a notch by filing a formal complaint. That way your concern is fully documented. Make sure to let the school know that you want a copy of that complaint put in the teacher's personnel file.

Starting a Records Binder

By the time you get to the point at which you are thinking about a special education referral for your child, you've probably already been fairly involved in your child's education. And if you've had problems with the teacher or school, you should already have a fair amount of paperwork. Keeping that paperwork in a records binder can help you store and organize that information so you know where all of it is whenever you need it.

ESSENTIAL

A records binder goes by many names in the special education community. You may hear it called an IEP binder, an IEP notebook, or even simply "the notebook." It is typically a three-ring binder divided into pertinent sections.

The first thing you need to do to create a records binder is to create a checklist of important papers and communication that you need to collect. The checklist following can be used as a guide to help you, and there's a blank copy in Appendix C at the end of this book.

Checklist of Items for a Records Binder

Once you've gathered all the information, place the checklist in the front of the binder to remind you of what's inside and what information you need to keep updated. The items on the list sort themselves pretty naturally into sections for your notebook, and if you don't have all of the items on the checklist, that's okay; just put what you do have in there and add to it as you need to.

○ Concerns about School-Related Issues chart (see Chapter 6 and Appendix C). You may want to keep blank copies in your binder, too.

○ School handbook and/or policy information and a school calendar

○ Medical information, including recent reports related to your child's disability as well as names and contact information for medical personnel

○ Contact information of services providers, evaluators, and school personnel

○ Reports cards, progress reports, and standardized test results

○ Awards and achievements your child has received. If you don't have certificates, make a list.

○ Communication logs and printed e-mails (see following section).

○ Letters and notes to and from the school and service providers.

○ Copy of the completed Referral for Evaluation and Consent to Evaluate forms

○ Copy of your *Parental Rights and Procedural Safeguards* (the parents' rights and responsibilities booklet)

○ Prior written notices for meetings.

○ Evaluation reports

○ Meeting notes and notices

○ 504 plans and accompanying documentation

○ Individualized educational program and associated documentation, including a behavior intervention plan (if your child has one)

○ Notices regarding disciplinary action and/or suspension notices

○ Samples of schoolwork, especially those that show improvement or struggle on your child's part

○ Blank notebook paper for taking notes

○ Other _____

Remember that a records binder is an ever-evolving record of your child's academic career, so you'll be continually adding to the binder. Keeping the records in chronological order can make this much easier. Also, even if your child's IEP or 504 plan is updated or revised, always keep the previous versions in your binder. You never know when you'll need to refer back to it.

Requesting Your Child's Records

If you don't have all of your child's records, that's okay. Whether or not your child has already been found eligible for special education, you have the right to review and get a copy of his educational record. If your child is in special education, this right is provided to you under IDEA, but if he's not, the Family Educational Rights and Privacy Act (known as FERPA) still gives you the legal right to your child's educational records.

Although IDEA regulations allow for school districts to charge you for copies of your child's record, the law also makes it clear that if that expense is a hardship that will keep you from looking at the records (and you can prove it), then the school cannot charge you.

FACT

Each state has varying regulations about how long the school has to provide you with your child's educational record after you request it. However, both IDEA and FERPA say records need to be provided within forty-five days, so any state deadline can only be shorter, not longer than that.

When you request your child's educational record, the request should be made in writing to the person in charge of special education and/or student records. Ask the school principal or call the superintendent's office to make sure you have the correct name and address to whom to send your request.

How to Write a Request for Records Letter

Your letter should include anything and everything that could possibly be a part of your child's record. Sometimes, schools use a variety of ways to store and categorize student information, so there could be information filed under your child's name, your name, her student ID number or social security number, or other unique identifier. When you send your letter, make it very clear that you want all the information, no matter how or where it's stored. Here's an example of what that might look like (and a sample copy can also be found in Appendix B).

Re: Request and Parental Consent for Student's Education Records

Dear Mr. Principal,

I am writing to request a copy of all school records pertaining to my child, Sally Y. I am requesting all education records that the school district has in relation to my child, no matter the location of these records within the school district, i.e., the special education office, central office, local school, or any other office or department. As provided for by §300.616 of the Individuals with Disabilities Education Improvement Act of 2004, I am also requesting a list of the "types and locations" of said education records.

This request is made under the provisions of the Family Educational Records and Privacy Act and IDEA 2004. It includes all records that contain personally identifiable information about Sally and us, Ima and Ura Y., using all identifiers the school district employs.

Included in this request are all tests, report cards, progress reports, incident reports, teacher and staff notes regarding my child including interoffice correspondence, communication log notes, meeting notes, observations, evaluations, notices for meetings, current and previous IEPs and 504 plans, and any records, in any format, not stated that pertain to my child.

I would really appreciate having these records within five days of your receipt of this letter. I will call you on (a date three days after anticipated receipt of letter) to make arrangements for picking up and/or copying these records.

Please feel free to contact me if you have questions. Thank you for your help.

Respectfully,
Ima and Ura Y.

Keeping a Communication Log

Having records, paperwork, and other documentation organized is a critical part of keeping involved in your child's education and being informed throughout the special education process. But sometimes there are important conversations or interactions that happen that aren't documented. Keeping a communication log is a very simple way of creating a paper trail in those types of situations. For example, if your child's teacher calls you to tell you his one-to-one aide is going to be out sick and the school doesn't have a replacement, that's a conversation worth documenting. It's not only a violation of his IEP, but if your child has a tough day without the aide, then you have documentation backing up that the aide was not there and that there wasn't a substitute. Here's how that might look:

▼ PARENT COMMUNICATION LOG

Date and Form of Contact	With Whom?	Initiated By:	Reason:	Discussion/ Outcome:
11/15/13, phone call	Classroom teacher Ms. X. and mother	Ms. X	1:1 aide absent	Ms. X. informed mother that 1:1 will be out today. No sub. Mother expressed concerns about how that will affect child's day.

Date and Form of Contact	With Whom?	Initiated By:	Reason:	Discussion/ Outcome:

As you can see, a communication log doesn't have to be complicated at all. It simply needs to have a way of documenting when you spoke to whom about what and the basic gist of the conversation. You can also record e-mails in your communication log, but since e-mail can be printed, a log lends itself better to documenting phone and in-person conversations.

Getting the Special Education Process Started

At this point you've got a solid base of information about your child—what she's struggling with in school, what your main concerns about her learning are—and you've expressed them to your child's teacher. Your child may be participating in a response-to-intervention program or have a 504 plan in place, but if she's still not where you think she should be academically, it's time to start the special education process. You have the right to make that request at any time, and now that you have a lot of information, it's a good time to do that.

How to Formally Request an Evaluation

Though your child's teacher can put in a referral for special education evaluation, if you have concerns about your child's learning, it's better to do it yourself. You can begin by calling the school and asking for the special education administrator or the IEP coordinator. Explain why you are calling and specifically use the words, "I am requesting that my child be evaluated for special education." Be sure to write down the details of the call in your communication log and then write and send a formal letter to follow up.

When you write the formal letter, refer back to your notes, any communications you've had from the school, your child's test scores, and report cards to make sure you're including as much specific information as possible about both what has and hasn't worked. This is where data collected via a response-to-intervention program, and conversations with your child's teacher about what has been tried in the classroom, come in very handy. Following is a sample letter to formally request to begin the special education process. A sample letter for your use can be found in Appendix B.

Dear Ms. Special Education Administrator,

I am writing to formally request that my child, Sally Y., be evaluated for special education services under the Child Find obligations of the Individuals with Disabilities Act (IDEA). I am asking that Sally be given a comprehensive educational assessment by the school district in regard to the concerns I have outlined below. I am also requesting that an IEP meeting be scheduled to discuss an evaluation and assessment plan that will be most appropriate to look at Sally's needs.

As part of this assessment process and conversation, I also would like to request that Sally be assessed under Section 504 of the Rehabilitation Act of 1973 to see whether she has a disability as defined by that law, and to identify what accommodations are needed in the general education classroom in the event she is not found eligible for special education services. For that reason, I would ask that the 504 coordinator be present at this initial meeting as well. Please note that I am not saying that I am comfortable substituting a 504 assessment for a special education assessment, only that I think both are an appropriate way to determine Sally's needs and disability.

I am concerned that Sally is struggling in school and may need special education support in order to learn best. Sally is in 2nd grade at Anytown School in Ms. X.'s class. More specifically, I am concerned that Sally is not learning to read as easily as the rest of her peers. She struggles with sounding out words, reading fluently, keeping her place when she reads, and being able to summarize and express thoughts about what she reads. I have spoken with Ms. X. on October 1, 2014, to discuss these concerns, and the following has been tried to help: small-group instruction, increased reading time at home, Reading Recovery instruction, and response-to-intervention programs.

Please feel free to call me for more information. I will follow up with you on (date three days after this letter will be received).

Respectfully,
Ima Y.

Note that while the letter requests that Sally be evaluated for special education services, it also asks for a simultaneous assessment of her rights under Section 504. That way, if Sally is found ineligible for special education services, the process to see if she qualifies for a 504 plan doesn't have to start all over.

CHAPTER 10

After a Referral Has Been Made

Having your child referred for a special education evaluation can be both a relief and a stressor. You know you've started the process to make your child's life at school a little easier, but you may worry about whether your child is going to feel singled out or if the evaluation process is going to be hard for her. Those are all things you can address before any evaluation even begins.

What Happens Now?

Within a week or so of writing your request for referral, you should be hearing from the school about setting up a prereferral meeting to discuss what types of assessment and evaluation will be most appropriate for assessing your child's needs or type of disability. In fact, once the referral has been written, IDEA has a fairly strict timeline to which all schools must adhere, but getting that timeline started is up to you.

ALERT

If you have not received any type of response within a week, make sure to call and follow up. Part of being your child's advocate means knowing that unless the ball is in motion, it's almost always in your court.

Once a referral has been initiated, the school has a tight deadline of fifteen days in which to notify you of a referral (if you didn't make it), develop an evaluation plan (also known as an assessment plan), inform you of the plan, and provide you with a copy of your *Parental Rights and Procedural Safeguards*. (That's the document that tells you not only what your rights are but also what steps to take if you feel they have been violated.)

The First Fifteen Days: An Evaluation Plan

All school districts deal with creating evaluation plans a little differently. Sometimes, if a child's needs are well known and have been the subject of a number of conferences between parents and the school, the school decides on a course of action, and parents are sent a copy of their *Parental Rights and Procedural Safeguards*, an evaluation plan, and Consent to Evaluate form. In other situations, a team of people who know and have worked with your child will sit down with you at a prereferral meeting to discuss which evaluations and assessments will be most helpful to include as a part of your child's comprehensive educational evaluation.

The Next Fifteen Days: Agreeing to the Plan

Whether there's a prereferral meeting or not, the school must provide you with a copy of the proposed evaluation plan and Consent to Evaluate form, either in person or by mail. Just because there's a plan for evaluation doesn't mean you have to agree to it, either. That's part of your rights—you can disagree with a proposed course of action at any time. However, you have fifteen days in which to make that decision. If you do not sign and return the form saying you agree with the plan and to having your child assessed, the special education process comes to a halt. That's why if you have concerns about the proposed plan, it's better to talk to the school to get more information or provide them with an alternate plan to discuss.

The Next Sixty Days: Evaluation, Reports, and Eligibility Meeting

Once you've signed the consent form, the clock really starts ticking for the school district. Within the next sixty calendar days, the school and its service providers must complete all assessments and evaluations, set up a meeting to discuss eligibility for special education services, provide you with at least five days prior written notice before the meeting, and provide you with copies of the evaluation reports at least two days before the scheduled meeting. That's a lot to do, especially if there's a shortage of evaluators and a number of students to assess!

FACT

In some states, if your child is absent for more than three days after the consent form has been signed, the school district is allowed to extend the timeline by the number of days your child was absent from school.

If you look at the timeline carefully, you'll notice that the whole process can actually take up to ninety days before you even sit down to talk about whether or not your child has been found eligible for special education services. If there's a school vacation longer than five days during that time, IDEA says the timeline can be put on hold during that period.

In order to keep track of the deadlines, it's a good idea to circle the date of the referral, and the date you provided consent, on the school calendar in your records binder. Then count out sixty days from the date of consent and circle it on the calendar. If you haven't been informed of any set evaluation times, or received any assessment paperwork to fill out within a month, it's a good idea to call the IEP coordinator to check in on how everything is proceeding.

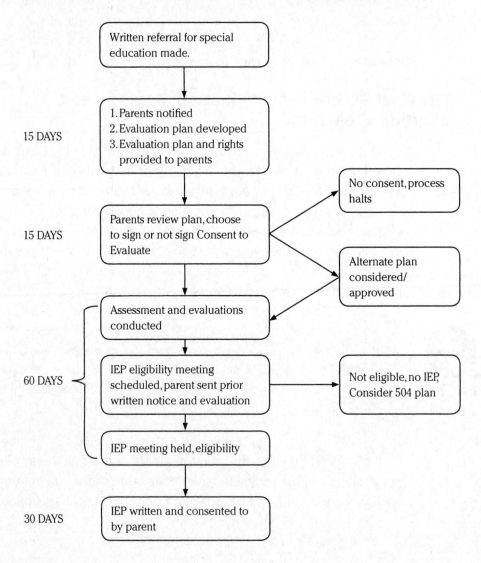

Written referral for special education made.

15 DAYS
1. Parents notified
2. Evaluation plan developed
3. Evaluation plan and rights provided to parents

No consent, process halts

15 DAYS
Parents review plan, choose to sign or not sign Consent to Evaluate

Alternate plan considered/ approved

Assessment and evaluations conducted

60 DAYS
IEP eligibility meeting scheduled, parent sent prior written notice and evaluation

Not eligible, no IEP, Consider 504 plan

IEP meeting held, eligibility

30 DAYS
IEP written and consented to by parent

The Difference Between an Evaluation and an Assessment

One of the things that can be confusing as your child is in the evaluation phase for special education is how many phrases are used interchangeably. It's not unusual for parents to be asked for their opinion on the assessment plan and then be sent an evaluation report in the mail. Though you may hear the terms "assessment" and "evaluation" used for the same purpose, it's worth knowing that under IDEA the two have very different meanings. The major difference between assessments and evaluations is what they are used for.

When IDEA talks about assessments, it's referring to the general—usually standardized—tests given to all students to evaluate the progress they are making toward the grade-level expectations of the school and state. That definition alone shows some of the reason the two ideas get confused. If an assessment is used to evaluate something, isn't it an evaluation? The short answer is not really.

An assessment looks at how students are doing at learning what they need to meet a specific goal. That goal is set for an entire age group as opposed to the individualized goals outlined in the plan of a child in special education. Assessments are used to measure what your child and his peers have learned or mastered in a particular area of study.

FACT

Just because assessments are given to all students doesn't mean they aren't helpful. The information collected about your child's progress can actually help document your child's need for special education.

On the other hand, evaluations are used to gather specific information about your child's current level of functioning and to get a better idea of how he processes information. Some of the evaluative information may be gathered from school-wide assessments, but it's also accompanied by observations and more specialized tests. Some of those tests provide a look at how your child's performance and abilities compare to other kids his age.

In this case, the purpose of all of this information gathering is not to see what your child knows but to figure out whether your child has problems with learning and in what areas. That evaluative data helps the team decide

125

if your child is eligible for special education services and which ones would be of help to him.

A Parent's Rights and Role in the Process

It may feel as though once the referral for special education has been made that things are sort of out of your hands and now it's up to the school, but your job as parental advocate is just beginning. You have rights that are provided to you and your child under the law, and you have responsibilities that aren't legally binding but are an important part of making sure you're staying involved in the process. Your rights and responsibilities in the evaluation phase include:

1. The right to approve, modify, or reject the evaluation plan, and the responsibility to ask for more information about parts of the plan you don't understand or about which you need more information.
2. The right to meet with the evaluator to discuss your observations and concerns about your child, and the responsibility to make your child available for evaluation so the school can meet the sixty-day timeline.
3. The right to have your child evaluated in his native language (or sign language, if applicable), and the responsibility to make sure the evaluator is aware of this need.
4. The right for your child to be evaluated by a trained professional in all areas in which disability is suspected, and the responsibility to ask about the evaluator's credentials and experience.

Preparing Your Child for Assessment

Sometimes, with all the paperwork and negotiation, it can be easy to overlook your child's role in evaluation for special education services. While you're working with the school to figure out how to make learning easier for her, she's the one who is struggling and will soon face a series of evaluations. No matter what her age, your child will need some explanation and preparation for what's going to happen. Here's what happened when John's parents neglected to provide some context for his visit with the psychological examiner.

ALERT

A school is no longer required to meet the sixty-day evaluation deadline if a parent "repeatedly fails" or "refuses to produce" his or her child for evaluation. (CFR 34, § 300.301)

John was a student whose diagnosis of anxiety disorder meant he had a 504 plan in place to make accommodations in the classroom. Those accommodations tried to address the frustration and anxiety that were causing emotional outbursts that had led, on occasion, to removal from the classroom and even suspension. As part of his 504 plan, John's teacher had implemented a behavior plan and chart, and had tried to develop some unobtrusive signals to help John see when it looked as though his frustration was mounting. The 504 plan wasn't particularly successful and his team decided a more comprehensive evaluation for special education was necessary.

John's parents brought him to the psychological examiner's office on the day of his evaluation, telling him simply that he had to go to an appointment to talk to somebody about his trouble at school. When the examiner asked John if he knew why he was there, John said it was because he was a bad kid who kept getting into trouble at school. Though the examiner tried to explain to John that he was, in actuality, there to help figure out why school was challenging to him and to find some ways to make it easier, John wasn't convinced. He was very guarded with the examiner and wouldn't talk very much.

As you can see, John didn't really know what the psychological examiner was going to do, nor did he understand that the adults in his life were concerned about why he was having trouble in school. He was under the impression that he somehow had brought this evaluation on himself by acting out or being a "bad kid."

Talking to your child about why you and his teachers are meeting is key in helping him understand the evaluation process. Knowing that everybody wants to figure out why he's having difficulty or experiencing frustration at school, and that they want to find ways to make it easier for him, can go a long way in easing his mind. Once he understands that, you can explain that in the next few weeks he may be taken out of class or brought to an appointment to do some activities that will help get a better sense of his abilities.

Younger children may understand this better if you couch it in terms of "special types of games," while older children are likely to understand the concept of testing. Just make sure you explain that these aren't the kinds of tests he can study for, nor should he worry about giving right or wrong answers. If John's parents had prepared him for assessment, the conversation he had could have gone much differently.

> John's parents explained to him that they had sat down with his teachers and the principal at his school because they were all worried about how frustrating school seemed to be for him. They explained that everybody was concerned because the things he and his teacher had been trying to help him with in the classroom didn't seem to be working as well as they had hoped, and that all the adults agreed they'd like to see if they could find better ways to help John.
>
> John's parents then told him that in order to figure that out, they needed the help of a person who specialized in looking at how kids learn and in suggesting ways to make learning easier for kids. This person, they explained, would need to talk with John and do some testing, but not the kind they do at the pediatrician's office. These tests would be tests that ask questions and play some games to learn how John thinks.
>
> When John arrived at the psychological examiner's office, and the examiner asked him if he knew why he was there, John was able to explain that he gets frustrated and has trouble in school. He went on to tell the examiner that his parents and teachers thought it would help to know more about how he learns to find new ways to help him at school. John was an informed and cooperative participant in the evaluation process, and the examiner was able to gather some very helpful data.

CHAPTER 11

The Evaluation and Assessment Process

You may feel comfortable in helping your child understand what is going to happen during an assessment, but that's not the same as you feeling comfortable that you understand the whole evaluation process. As you know, your child's school must provide you with *prior written notice* of their plan to evaluate and with an evaluation plan. Knowing what IDEA requires to be part of a comprehensive evaluation can make it much easier for you to decide whether the proposed evaluation plan is something you agree with.

The Basic Components of an Evaluation

One of the things that can make it easier to understand the evaluation process your child has to go through to see if he's eligible for special education is to stop thinking of the word "evaluation" as meaning the same thing as the word "test." The reason it's known as an evaluation *process* is because it's a whole series of steps that are taken to look at (or evaluate) your child's strengths and weaknesses and how he's performing academically. The process is an evaluation to get a better understanding about all of the things about your child, which can't happen by doing just one assessment or test. That's why IDEA talks about a comprehensive evaluation.

A comprehensive evaluation looks at all the aspects of your child that could be contributing to his trouble with school. Ideally, there will be tests, observations, or other ways of assessing your child's health, vision, hearing, social and emotional development, overall intelligence, academic performance, communication skills, and motor skills. Of course, if some of these things have already been tested or there's no concern about them—for example, if your child already passed a hearing screening—those elements don't have to be included in the comprehensive evaluation.

FACT

IDEA says that every child must have a full and complete (comprehensive) evaluation because one measurement doesn't provide enough information to create an entire individualized education program.

Because of all the areas that have to be looked at to determine if your child has a disability that makes him eligible for special education services, a comprehensive evaluation is made up of a number of different things. Those may include:

- A psychological evaluation that looks at and gathers information about your child's overall intelligence, strengths and weakness in learning, what his needs are in terms of how to be taught, and his social-emotional well-being and makeup

- Interviews with you and your child's teacher to get a detailed look at your child's social and academic history
- A physical exam to assess vision, hearing, and general health
- An observation of your child in his general education classroom
- An educational evaluation designed to look at areas of suspected disability. This evaluation may include new tests that measure your child's academic abilities and needs, as well as include information from school-wide assessments he has already participated in
- A functional behavioral assessment (FBA) to get a better understanding of reasons behind behavioral issues. An FBA includes detailed rating scales, checklists, and questionnaires for parents and teachers to give them the opportunity to provide information about how different people see your child's functional skills
- Speech/language evaluations and physical and/or occupational evaluations, if necessary
- A one-to-one interview with your child and important people in his life (most often these are his parents)

An evaluation may also include educational information that is already part of your child's record. His school records contain important information about how he's doing in school now and how he has done in the past. For instance, his scores on assessments, reports and data from response-to-intervention programs, report cards, samples of classroom work, and even discipline write-ups all provide really important information about how your child is functioning in school. When all of that available information is added to the results of the other tests and observations, it can help round out the picture of your child's abilities.

Know What IDEA Requires

On top of all the pieces that make up a comprehensive assessment, there are also some things that IDEA legally requires as part of an initial evaluation. Many of the requirements—like making sure that any tests are given in the language or form of communication your child understands best—are in place to make sure your child is evaluated fairly and that the results are as accurate as possible. Other IDEA requirements about evaluation include:

- All tests must be given by a professional trained in administering that test and who is knowledgeable in the skill area being looked at.
- An evaluation must gather information about all of the "areas of suspected disability."
- The end result must provide useful and relevant information that can be used to help make decisions about your child's educational needs and future program.

What's an Evaluation Plan?

The way the school plans to meet those requirements and gather information about your child's educational needs and possible disability is called an *evaluation plan*. The evaluation plan is the paper that tells you all of the tests the school wants to do and all of the other things that will be looked at to see if your child is eligible for special education. This is the plan you need to look over before giving your permission to have your child evaluated, either by signing a Consent to Evaluate form or by signing off on the plan itself.

ALERT

If you do not receive a written evaluation plan within fifteen days of your child being referred for special education, get in touch with the school and ask for one. Do not sign a consent form before fully reviewing what you are agreeing to!

In some school districts, parents take part in creating the evaluation plan during a meeting known as a pre-evaluation meeting. This meeting is not, however, a required part of the special education determination process. The evaluation plan is a requirement though, as is something known as "informed consent." Informed consent means that you need to completely understand what you are giving your permission for. It is the school's responsibility to explain all the pieces of the evaluation plan to you, including what each test is designed to look at and what type of professional will perform the test.

Sometimes school personnel won't always explain it to you in detail, not necessarily out of ill will, but because they don't always remember that not all parents are familiar with the special education process and testing. If you don't understand something on the evaluation plan, make sure to ask for more information before giving your permission for your child to be evaluated.

What's Included in an Evaluation Plan

An evaluation plan doesn't have to look a certain way or be on a specific form, but it does have to include certain information. You should be on the lookout for the plan to have a section that describes the areas in which your child is having difficulty and a place for questions that the team would like to try to answer through evaluation. This may include information about what disability is suspected or already known.

Additionally an evaluation plan will name the tests, assessments, and observations the school would like to perform, have a place for you to provide your approval (or disapproval), and give you the option to request other tests or types of evaluations.

Evaluating the Evaluation Plan

The option to disapprove or ask for other tests isn't just a formality. Just because the school comes up with an evaluation plan doesn't mean you have to agree with it or that it's the best plan for your child. That's where informed consent and seeking out advice is very helpful. Talk to your child's doctor, other parents, your child's teacher, or other people familiar with the proposed testing (and your child) if you're not sure about what the proposed plan means or whether it will give an accurate and full picture of your child. The questions you need to be able to answer before agreeing to an evaluation plan are:

- Are these tests the right ones to figure out if my child has the suspected disability?
- What is each test designed to measure?
- In what format is the test given?
- What will the results of the tests look like (i.e., will they have a numeric score or provide a written narrative of how my child did?)
- Will each test, observation, or assessment help to find ways for my child to learn better?
- Will these tests provide recommendations for what services, programs, or accommodations will help my child?

- Is there a specific purpose for a classroom observation, and will it be done during a subject that my child is having difficulty with?
- What experience and training does the named evaluator have?
- Who is the evaluator who will be working with my child?

Once you have answers to those questions, you can make a decision about whether you agree with the plan or not. If you think the plan is okay, sign where indicated and give it back to the school with an attached sticky note asking for a copy. That copy should then become a part of your child's records binder.

What to Do If You Don't Agree with the Plan

If you don't agree with the evaluation plan, make sure you're able to put into words what you don't like about it. You have the legal right to ask for changes, ask that additional tests or information be included, or to flat out reject the plan, but if you're not specific in your reasons why, it's less likely that the school district is going to be willing to make changes.

For example, if there is concern that your child is having trouble filtering out distractions in the classroom, the evaluation plan may include psychological testing to look for or rule out ADHD, but it may not include an occupational therapist assessing your child's response to sensory input. Since ADHD and sensory integration issues often have overlapping symptoms, you may feel as though the evaluation plan does not address all the "areas of suspected disability."

Accepting a Plan Doesn't Have to Be All or Nothing

Luckily, you have more options than to take it or leave it when it comes to evaluation plans. In fact, just because you disagree with some of it or think it's not complete doesn't mean you can't consent to the pieces you do agree with. If you're not in total agreement with the plan, you have a few options: You can accept the plan with conditions, ask that a new plan be developed, or reject the plan outright. Keep in mind that if you reject an evaluation plan, the school district is not required to come up with a new one of which you approve.

ALERT

Though it rarely happens, if the school feels strongly that the evaluation plan you've rejected is appropriate, they can ask for mediation or go to a due process hearing to ask for the right to evaluate without your consent.

If you are rejecting the plan in full, check off the box that says you do not give your permission to test your child and attach a letter explaining your reasoning. You can find a sample letter in Appendix B. In part, your letter might look like the following:

Dear Mr. IEP Coordinator,

I am writing to express my concerns about the proposed special education evaluation plan for my child, Sally Y., which I received on October 1, 2014. I have examined the plan in detail and do not feel it really addresses all of the issues Sally is having. As the plan stands, I am unable to accept it.

While I am in agreement that the Wechsler Intelligence Scale for Children (WISC) would be helpful in determining Sally's intelligence, I don't think the rest of the proposed tests or included information will provide a reliable and full picture of Sally's needs and abilities. For instance, teacher notes, disciplinary action letters, and report card comments cannot be considered in place of a formal classroom observation by a trained professional.

I also feel that additional testing is needed in the area of sensory processing. I am formally requesting that an occupational therapy evaluation to determine her sensory profile be added to the evaluation plan.

Lastly, I am uncomfortable with the fact that the evaluation plan does not have anything in it about my husband and I having a chance to express our thoughts about what we see as Sally's strengths and weakness, either through questionnaires or a conversation with the evaluator.

I look forward to hearing from you in the next week as to setting up a meeting to draft a new evaluation plan. I am available to meet about this matter at your convenience.

Thank you.

Sincerely,
Ima Y.

How to Request Changes

Accepting the plan with conditions means that you want additional information or testing considered, you don't want your child to undergo some of the proposed testing, or some combination of those two things. In any of those cases, the best thing to do is to provide your consent for the parts of the plan you do accept. Attach a letter indicating what you are providing permission for and outlining any additional testing or information you would like considered. If the evaluation plan does not have a separate line for you to sign for each proposed action, be sure to cross out the things you are not consenting to before signing the form. Your letter might look something like this (a sample letter can be found in Appendix B):

Dear Mr. IEP Coordinator,

I am writing in regard to the proposed special education evaluation plan for my child, Sally Y., which I received on October 1, 2014. I have examined the plan in detail and am prepared to accept the plan conditionally.

While I am in agreement that the Wechsler Intelligence Scale for Children (WISC), a classroom observation, and the Conners' Rating Scales would be helpful, respectively, in determining Sally's intelligence, getting a sense of her functioning in the classroom, and assessing the likelihood of ADHD, I don't think that the plan proposes to evaluate every area of suspected disability.

I believe additional testing is needed in the area of sensory processing to determine whether her distractibility is related to sensory issues. I am formally requesting that an occupational therapy evaluation be added to the plan to determine her sensory profile.

Furthermore, after some investigation, I do not feel that the tests on the list—other than those I have mentioned—will provide reliable information, and I do not give my permission for them to be administered.

I look forward to hearing from you in the next week as to how you wish to proceed. I am available to meet about this matter at your convenience.

Thank you.

Sincerely,
Ima Y.

Talking to the Evaluator

Once there's an evaluation plan in place for your child, you'll have a better sense of what kinds of testing will be done and who will be doing each piece of the evaluation. But you might not always know when the testing will take place. If your school district has on-staff evaluators, it will be much easier for the testing to be done during the regular school day, which means you may not be given much (if any) notice as to when your child will be evaluated. That's as opposed to a situation in which your school contracts with outside providers; in that case you may be contacted to schedule an appointment with your child.

You may think that you've done your part by expressing your concerns about your child and getting an evaluation plan in place, but you should also take the time to talk to the evaluator (or evaluators). Your child's teacher and some of the other school staff know what you're worried about, but until the referral for evaluation showed up on the evaluator's desk, she probably hasn't had any knowledge of or information about your child. All the information she has is in the paperwork the school has provided.

Ask the evaluator if she has time to meet with you before she tests your child so that you can discuss what the testing involves, what it will show, and what happens after it is done. It may not always be easy to get an evaluator to meet with you; by law she's not obligated to and technically she works for the school district, which may make her more wary of seeming as though she is taking sides against the school.

If an evaluator will not meet with you in person, ask her if she can spare some time to speak with you on the phone. Keep calm, stay reasonable, and continue to express that you want to speak with her about how the tests work and that you'd like to provide her with your perspective on your child and his struggles.

ESSENTIAL

Whether or not you get the chance to meet with an evaluator, it's always wise to send a letter that states your concerns in an objective manner. It gives an evaluator a balanced view of your child, and the letter becomes part of your child's evaluation file, should you need it to contest the evaluation report.

It's about Your Child's Best Interests

Taking the time to get in touch with evaluators before testing takes place is a good idea for a few reasons: It gives you a chance to provide the evaluator with some insight about your child, relate your concerns about your child directly to the evaluator, and develop a positive relationship with the evaluator. It's important that her impression of you isn't based on information she gets from other people.

Building a positive relationship with the evaluator can only help your child. Not only will it let your child know that you trust the person who will be doing his assessment, but the evaluator is the person who will be looking at your child's abilities and, in the end, writing the report that will help determine whether your child is eligible for special education services.

Developing a good rapport gives you a chance to show the evaluator that your main concern is your child and that you have your child's best interests in mind. It can give you the opportunity to help the evaluator see your child as a real person, not just numbers on a test or information in a file. And the more comfortable you are with the evaluator (and the evaluator with you), the more readily you can talk about what you think your child's educational needs are.

ESSENTIAL

If you've had a tough time getting the school to evaluate your child, there's always the possibility that someone has mistaken your advocacy as difficultness or pushiness. That's not the impression you want an evaluator to have of you, so reaching out can help her see you as the advocate you are.

It's a balancing act to make sure you're telling the evaluator exactly what you want her to know about your child and what you think that means in terms of your child's education without sounding as though you're telling the evaluator how to do her job. But it's a balancing act well worth attempting because it's important that your concerns make it into the final evaluation report.

For instance, saying, "I'd like your report to recommend that Sally not get services in the resource room and that she should have a one-to-one aide," can be off-putting, so if it's the information you want to convey, you'll have to do it in a different way. Try something a little less direct, such as "In her last written progress report, Sally's teacher said she thinks Sally is able to learn in the general education classroom with some consistent extra assistance."

The Evaluation Report

Once all the testing is finished, each evaluator will write a report detailing all the information gathered. Sometimes an evaluator will write a first draft of the report and let you take a look at it to make sure any information you provided is accurately recorded and summarized, but often there will only be a final report issued.

The report will have a lot of information in it and can be overwhelming to wade through. Luckily, most reports have a summary and/or conclusions section at the end that summarizes what the evaluator has learned and what it all means. If you are overwhelmed by the report when you get it, flip to that summary, read it first, and then go back through the entire report piece by piece.

A thorough evaluation report will include a statement about the reason your child was referred, background information about your child's social and academic history, a list of the tests performed and the information the evaluator reviewed, a summary of the test results, an interpretation of what those test results mean in terms of educational needs, a diagnosis (if one can be made), and a section of recommendations.

The recommendations section will have the evaluator's thoughts on what types of educational accommodations, programs, and related services your child would benefit from. It may also suggest other tests that should be done to get more information about your child. Or, if the evaluator didn't find any signs of a disability, the recommendations section might simply say, "No services recommended."

Reviewing the Report

By law the school and evaluator are not required to provide you with a copy of the evaluation report before an IEP eligibility meeting. But the report must be made available to you at least two days before the meeting and a copy given to you at that meeting or not more than ten days after it.

If that sounds confusing, that's because it is. Basically, what all that means is that the school doesn't have to give you your *own* copy of an evaluation report to look over before an IEP meeting, but it does have to let you look at one, even if it means you do it sitting in a conference room at the school. However, once you're at an IEP meeting, you have to be given a copy of all of the reports that are being used to decide whether your child is eligible for special education services.

Most of the time, though, getting a copy of the report before an IEP eligibility meeting isn't a problem; often it's just a matter of telling the evaluator or special education staff ahead of time that you'd like a copy sent to you when the report is finished. It's actually to everybody's benefit for you to have a chance to look it over before a meeting.

QUESTION

Why would my child's school refuse to give me a copy of the reports before a meeting?
A school might withhold the evaluation report if they are concerned you will disagree with it or that you might use the information to support the need for services they are not willing or prepared to provide.

It can save time if you all have had a chance to look over the information and recommendations. If you've had the opportunity to reach out to the school or evaluator to have any questions answered before a meeting, you're taking less time to discuss what the report means and more time to discuss whether it means your child has a disability and is eligible for special education services.

If You Disagree with the Report

Sometimes after reading an evaluation report, there may be things you don't agree with. If it's something minor, like a few details the evaluator got wrong about your family or your child, there's nothing wrong with contacting and asking the evaluator directly to issue a corrected version of the report.

If, however, you disagree with the results or recommendations, that's different. In that case, it's important to be clear about what you are disputing. If you have concerns about the recommendations the evaluator made, that is something you can discuss in depth at the IEP eligibility meeting. If the IEP team agrees that other services are needed or what the evaluator recommended isn't appropriate, the team has the power to make that decision. Remember, an IEP addresses your child's individual needs in the way the IEP team decides is best.

If you're concerned that the test results aren't valid, it's a good idea to make sure you know the scope and limitations of the test(s) the evaluator used. You can do this either by contacting the evaluator and asking to meet with him so he can explain the test in detail or by asking the IEP coordinator to sit down with you and talk it over.

Once you understand the test, if you still feel as though it's inaccurate, send a letter to the IEP coordinator and evaluator expressing your concerns. Include a copy of the evaluation report, highlight the information that you dispute, and include your suggestions as to how to remedy the problem. If you want the evaluator to reevaluate your child using another test, be specific in saying so. The school may not agree to your request, but at least your concerns are in writing and on file.

You can also choose to have your child evaluated by an independent evaluator, one who is not associated with or employed by the school district. Should you choose to do so, IDEA requires that the IEP team discuss the evaluation. However, IDEA does *not* say that the school district has to accept the results and recommendations of a parent-obtained evaluation. If you choose to have your child evaluated independently, you may want to consider formally requesting an Independent Educational Evaluation. When you make this request, the school may be required to pay for the evaluation. Chapter 15 provides you with in-depth information about how to request an Independent Educational Evaluation at the school's expense and how to find an evaluator to complete such an evaluation.

CHAPTER 12

What You Need to Know about Testing

There are a number of different tests that can be used to determine your child's level of functioning, and they don't all measure the same thing, which is why it's important to know what a test is trying to measure before you decide whether or not you think the results are accurate. The type of disability your child has or the area in which she's having problems learning will help determine the tests that will be done to gather supporting evidence about her educational abilities.

What Is an IQ?

One type of test that is almost always completed as part of a comprehensive evaluation is a test to determine your child's intelligence, which is often referred to as an IQ. It is a common misperception that IQ and intelligence mean the same thing.

FACT

IQ stands for "intelligence quotient," which is a simply the name given to the score of an intelligence test.

Your child's IQ is a number score, but her intelligence is her ability to learn, adapt to situations, and problem-solve. Intelligence is about how your child thinks, what she knows, how she is able to learn, how she stores information, and how she applies what she learns and knows to everyday situations.

IQ versus Intelligence

Your child's IQ score, or the results of intelligence testing, can provide insight into her ability to use previously learned information to help solve different, but similar, problems. This is known as "transferring" information, and some disabilities make it very difficult for children to transfer information from one situation to another, because they don't see how the two situations are related. For example:

> One of the goals in kindergarten was for Samantha and her classmates to be able to recognize color words. To help make this easier in the beginning of the year, every time the teacher wrote the colors words, she wrote them in the appropriate color. "R-E-D" was always written with a red marker, "G-R-E-E-N" was always written with a green marker, and so on. All of the children seemed to learn their color words quickly, including Samantha, but when the teacher starting writing the words in black marker, Samantha couldn't read them anymore. She had learned to read those words in a certain color and was unable to recognize that the letter combinations were the same regardless of the color in which they were written.

Samantha's inability to see this wasn't dependent on the number of her IQ, but rather on her ability to transfer knowledge from one situation to another to solve a related problem. The way she thinks and processes information is part of her intelligence, the strengths and weaknesses of which can be looked at by in-depth intelligence testing.

Intelligence is influenced by a number of things, including genetics and environment. Some children's intelligence or ability to learn is limited by genetic disorders such as Down syndrome or phenylketonuria. Sometimes a child's intelligence is affected by environmental factors, such as exposure to lead paint, and sometimes an accident or injury that causes damage to the brain affects intelligence.

FACT

Being raised in a nonstimulating environment without being exposed to learning experiences can affect a child's intelligence, but the effect is less permanent, especially if the child is still young when she is exposed to new experiences and learning opportunities.

Because your child continues to build her base of knowledge as she gets older and is exposed to more ideas and learning, her IQ score may not always be as accurate if she's tested as a preschooler or early elementary-age student. The older she gets, the more likely her IQ is to stay in the same range.

Calculating IQ

At its simplest, you can look at your child's IQ as her mental age divided by her chronological age, which is known as her "mental quotient." The mental quotient is then multiplied by 100 to obtain an IQ score. Chronological age is easy to figure out—it's how old your child is. Mental age is more difficult to determine, which is what intelligence testing is designed to do. It looks at your child's ability to perform tasks and solve problems that children in her age range should be able to do.

If your child's mental age is the same as her chronological age, then she will have an IQ of 100, which is considered to be an average IQ. If her mental age is younger than her chronological age, her IQ will fall in the below-average range, and if her mental age is more than her chronological age, she will have an above-average IQ. Assuming your child's chronological age is fifteen years old (CA=15), here's how that can look in all those situations:

ESSENTIAL

Your child's chronological age isn't rounded up or down; it's expressed in years and months. If your child is a month away from her seventh birthday, her chronological age is 6.11, or six years, eleven months.

▼ **MENTAL AGE ÷ CHRONOLOGICAL AGE = MENTAL QUOTIENT × 100 = INTELLIGENCE QUOTIENT**

Average: 15 (MA) ÷ 15 (CA) = 1 (MQ) × 100 = 100 IQ
Below Average: 12 (MA) ÷ 15 (CA) = .80 (MQ) × 100 = 80 IQ
Above Average: 17 (MA) ÷ 15 (CA) = 1.33 (MQ) × 100 = 133 IQ

Of course, it's not really that simple because intelligence tests look at a number of different areas of ability, so your child may do very well with verbal tasks and not as well with visual tasks. This means her score on the verbal portion of an IQ test may be much higher than her visual score. Averaged together, these scores indicate an overall intelligence score, but the information that she has more trouble learning visually is what's important when it comes to creating a special education program.

IQ Ranges

When you're sitting around the table for an IEP meeting and the professionals start talking about IQ ranges and standard scores, it can be overwhelming to understand what it all means. What you need to know about IQ scores is that they are reported on a standard scale, one that stays the same no matter what test is used, and a scale on which 100 is always the middle or the "norm."

Think of it like a thermometer on which 100 degrees Celsius is always the boiling point of water. The numbers always mean the same thing, and no matter what thermometer you use, when water starts to boil it will always measure 100 degrees. Anything higher than 100 degrees is still boiling. Anything lower than 100 degrees is not boiling, but the closer it gets to 100 degrees, the closer it is to boiling.

An IQ scale works the same way in that 100 is always exactly the middle. No matter how many people you give an IQ test to, exactly half of the group would score somewhere above 100 and exactly half would score somewhere below 100. The majority of people fall between the 85 to 115 ranges, though, so that whole range is considered average intelligence. It's above and below those numbers where professionals start making predictions about what your child's IQ means in terms of his ability to learn. The table here shows you which scores fall into which range and the possible implications for learning.

▼ IQ RANGES AND LEARNING IMPLICATIONS*

Standard Score	IQ Range	Learning Implications
69 and below	Extremely low	Mastering basic academic concepts will be difficult. Children are likely to need special education services to support basic learning and skills of daily living.
70–79	Borderline	Generalizing information from one learning situation to another may be very hard; children may learn best in a highly structured environment with much repetition of skills. The older children get, the more challenging learning may become due to increasing demands for abstract thinking.
80–89	Low average	There may be scattered strengths and weaknesses of skills and a need for closer monitoring of ongoing progress. Some extra learning support may be needed.
90–109; 110–119	Average; high average	A normal ability to learn is indicated. Academic troubles should be further investigated to see if there are specific areas in which a learning disability, behavioral disorder, or other concerns may be causing difficulty with processing and applying information.
120–129; 130 and above	Superior; very superior	Academic support may be needed in regard to enrichment and gifted learning programs.

*The language and scores used for educational classification and purposes differ slightly from the language and scores used for medical classification
(Source: Wilmshurst, Linda, and Alan W. Brue. *The Complete Guide to Special Education: Expert Advice on Evaluations, IEPs, and Helping Kids Succeed*. 2nd Edition, Jossey-Bass, 2011.)

Tests Used to Measure Intelligence

Evaluators don't always use the same test to measure intelligence. In choosing the test or tests to use with your child, the evaluator will take into consideration what will provide the most accurate information about your child. If, for example, your child has significant speech and language difficulties, using a test that relies heavily on verbal participation will provide a skewed view of your child's abilities. A test that has a way of measuring the same information without an emphasis on verbal communication would be more in line with your child's needs.

The Differential Ability Scale

The Differential Ability Scale has both a preschool and a school-age level, making it appropriate to use with children between the ages of two and half years up to seventeen years and eleven months old. The overall test has twenty subtests that look at your child's cognitive abilities and achievement in the areas of verbal, spatial, and nonverbal reasoning; memory; visual recognition; and processing of information. It is a good test to use with children with language difficulties because it has a specific nonverbal portion to it. The results are reported as a General Conceptual Ability (GCA).

Universal Nonverbal Intelligence Test (UNIT)

The Universal Nonverbal Intelligence Test is designed for use with children between the ages of five and seventeen years old. It is a good test to use with children with speech and language problems, hearing impairments, children for whom English is a second language, and/or children for whom verbal communication is a problem. The entire test is given and answered using a series of eight hand and body gestures such as pointing. UNIT measures memory and reasoning abilities.

Wechsler Intelligence Scales (WISC and WPPSI)

The Wechsler Intelligence Scales are some of the most commonly used tests for intelligence testing. The Wechsler Preschool and Primary Scale of Intelligence (WPPSI) can be used to test children aged two and a half years to seven years and three months old, while the Wechsler Intelligence Scale for Children (WISC) can be used for children ages six to sixteen years and eleven months old.

The WISC tests verbal comprehension, perceptual reasoning, working memory, and processing speed, using both language and symbol-based questions. This allows for an evaluator to see if there's a difference in how your child performs on language-based tasks than she does on spatial tasks. Each component of the test has its own score, and a full-scale IQ based on all of the information is provided, too.

Stanford-Binet Intelligence Scale

The Stanford-Binet isn't broken into different tests for different ages; the test is used with preschool children, school-age children, and adults. It looks at five different things: the ability to solve new problems, what information is already known, the ability to reason with numbers, visual-spatial reasoning and processing, and working memory (sometimes known as "mental manipulation"). The information is used to provide both a verbal IQ score and a nonverbal IQ score.

What Other Things Can Be Assessed?

Intelligence isn't the only thing that needs to be assessed when your child is being evaluated for special education services. It's helpful in giving information about what your child's level of functioning is, and in what ways she learns best, but it doesn't always address the issue of concern. There are other reasons that children are referred for evaluation, too, including (but not limited to) behavioral concerns, speech and language problems, problems with motor skills, or concerns about ADHD or autism. There are a number of other evaluation tools that can help provide information about your child's functioning.

Functional Behavioral Assessment

A functional behavioral assessment, or FBA, isn't a specific test; it's the term used for all of the things that are done to look closely at the cause and triggers of your child's inappropriate behaviors. Figuring out causes, patterns, and triggers for behavior can help the IEP team create a plan for dealing with the behavior.

There are a number of things that can be used as a part of an FBA, including parent and teacher rating scales (questionnaires that ask you to rate the severity and frequency of the troubling behaviors) and detailed observation of what occurs before, during, and after the behavior. This type of observation is often recorded on what is known as an ABC chart, a tool that can be just as useful at home as it is in the classroom.

ESSENTIAL

Ideally, the behavioral intervention plan developed from the information provided by a functional behavioral assessment should be positive and proactive as opposed to containing only negative consequences and reactive solutions. That way your child isn't always feeling punished and is being helped to learn new behavioral strategies.

An ABC chart looks at the antecedent (the circumstances or triggering situation that occurs right before the behavior), the behavior (what your child does or how she reacts), and the consequences (what happens as a result of the behavior). Keeping an ABC chart for several days to a couple of weeks can help uncover patterns in behavior. Let's take John, for example.

John was a bright student with anxiety disorder who, though he was on track academically, was having frequent emotional outbursts at school that would disrupt his learning and that of his classmates. These outbursts were both verbal and physical, and neither his teacher nor his parents had an explanation for what was causing them. John wasn't able to express why he was behaving in an inappropriate manner, nor was he very willing to talk about the outbursts. His teacher decided to keep an ABC chart to keep track of his behavior, and it revealed some interesting patterns.

There's a blank Antecedent, Behavior, Consequence chart in Appendix C, but here's what John's chart looked like:

▼ **JOHN'S ANTECEDENT, BEHAVIOR, CONSEQUENCE CHART (ABC CHART)**

Where did this occur?	Antecedent (What happened before the behavior occurred?)	Behavior (Describe what your child did, how he reacted, etc.)	Consequence (Describe what happened as a result of the behavior.)
In the gym.	Students were lining up to return to the classroom.	John pushed another child and yelled about how the child was in his way.	John was asked to leave the line and return to the classroom after the rest of the students.
In the lunchroom.	Students were sitting down at tables and eating lunch.	John got angry with another student for talking louder than the rules allowed for. He got very loud himself, pushing his chair away from the table.	John was asked to apologize, but refused to. He was not allowed to return to the table with his friends because of refusal.
On the playground.	Students were playing kickball and John was asked to move out of the way so another child could take his turn.	John got very upset, insisting it was his turn. When the teacher asked him to move, he insisted she wasn't listening to him and escalated into a verbal tantrum and throwing rocks.	John was suspended from school.

After looking more carefully at John's ABC chart, it became apparent that most of John's outbursts were occurring not during class time but during transitions and nonacademic time, and often in relation to his dealings with other students. This information, along with a classroom observation and parent and teacher rating scales, was helpful in pinpointing what kinds of things John was having trouble with, and in creating a behavioral intervention plan to help him learn new ways to react.

Childhood Autism Rating Scale (CARS)

CARS is a fairly simple rating scale used to help determine whether a child may have an autism spectrum disorder. It's a series of questions about how your child communicates, relates to other people, uses objects, and level of activity. It can be used to rate the behaviors of children ages two and up and is an assessment tool, not an evaluation. If CARS indicates that your child has characteristics that are more common to autism than other developmental delays, an evaluator is likely to recommend more in-depth evaluation.

Peabody Picture Vocabulary Test

The Peabody Picture Vocabulary Test—or the PPVT-4, as it is in its fourth edition—is a short test that can evaluate your child's receptive language and vocabulary. Your child will be given an image card with four pictures on it; the evaluator will say a word, and your child needs to point to the correct image. The test consists of more than 200 vocabulary items that increase in difficulty.

Clinical Evaluation of Language Fundamentals (CELF)

CELF is a test that can be used to evaluate the language skills for children ages five to twenty-one years old. In contrast to the PPVT-4, this test examines your child's understanding and use of language, not her vocabulary. It looks at a number of different aspects of language including word meaning, the ability to remember and retrieve words, the structure of sentences, and the ability to get the gist of what is being said or read to your child.

Vineland Adaptive Behavior Scale

The Vineland Adaptive Behavior Scale is filled out by parents, caregivers, and teachers to help assess your child's adaptive functioning skills. It's a fairly extensive questionnaire that asks you to rate your child's abilities and behaviors in the areas of communication, daily living, socialization, motor skills, and, sometimes, maladaptive behaviors (problematic behaviors that interfere with everyday life).

The Vineland Scale is particularly helpful in assessing the possibility of developmental delays, intellectual disabilities, and autism, as well as providing a very accurate picture of your child's strengths and weaknesses in activities of daily living. The questions often ask about the same thing in different ways to help make sure your answers are valid and consistent.

Conners' Parent and Teacher Rating Scales

The Conners' Rating Scales is a thorough assessment tool designed to look at the likelihood that your child's behaviors and learning difficulties are due to or related to ADHD. There are long- and short-form versions of the scales, which can be completed in a paper and pencil version or on a computer. The questions are given to parents and teachers, and there is a self-report for older children as well. All the information is gathered, scored, and then summarized to give a full and accurate picture of how what everybody is seeing fits together.

Advocating for a Truly Comprehensive Evaluation

As you can see, a comprehensive evaluation is a very involved process, or at least it should be. If your child's evaluation plan doesn't involve a number of different ways to look at her learning difficulties, it's not because there aren't enough options for testing. Now that you know more about the tests that are available and what they measure, you can be a more critical evaluator yourself. If you think one of these tools would provide helpful information, do not hesitate to talk to the IEP team, especially if the testing that has been done hasn't provided enough data to help determine eligibility for special education services.

CHAPTER 13

Is Your Child Eligible for Special Education?

From the day you give consent for evaluation of your child, the school district has sixty calendar days in which to have your child evaluated, provide the evaluation reports for review, and hold an eligibility meeting. At that meeting, you will sit down with the other IEP team members to go over the information that has been gathered and discuss whether your child is eligible for special education and related services.

Tips to Prepare for an Eligibility Meeting

Getting prepared for your child's eligibility meeting is something you can start doing during the evaluation process. That's the perfect time to make sure you've requested and reviewed your child's educational records and started a records binder.

FACT

Requesting and reviewing your child's records are actually two different rights given to you under FERPA. You can review the records at school to make sure you were given everything in the copies you requested.

Once the evaluations are complete, there are some other steps to take before you walk into a meeting.

Request and Review Evaluation Reports

Read everything in depth and reach out to the evaluators or school to ask for clarification about anything you don't understand. As you read, have a highlighter handy to mark statements you think support your child's eligibility. Most importantly, look at the recommendations to see if the evaluator specifically recommends your child be found eligible for or would benefit from special education services.

Follow Up with the School about Recommendations

If the evaluator has recommended special education services, you need to know whether or not the school agrees with that. Speak with the special education administrator or IEP coordinator and ask the question, making sure to log the conversation in your communication log. If the school will support the recommendation, that's the time to make a request for a joint eligibility and initial IEP development meeting, sometimes known as a program meeting. A sample letter for requesting a joint-purpose meeting can be found in Appendix B.

QUESTION

Why should I ask for a joint eligibility and IEP development meeting? If you know everyone is in agreement that your child is eligible for services and don't anticipate disagreement about what those services should be, a joint meeting can help your child get services sooner. Otherwise, you may have to wait at least another month before services are determined and started.

Prepare Your Case for Eligibility

Should the evaluation report not specifically recommend special education, the school is not willing to tell you whether they agree with a recommendation for services, or the school tells you they are recommending against special education, you need to be prepared to make your case that your child should be found eligible. Here are some ways to start doing that:

- **Gather your evidence.** This is where having already read the reports and your child's education record in depth will serve you well. You already know what information is available to support your child's need for special education services; you just need to put it together all in one place.

- **Find people who agree with you.** You have talked to many people along the way about your child's struggles. Whether it's your child's teachers, an evaluator, or a pediatrician, speak with whomever you know agrees with you and ask them to attend the eligibility meeting to support your position. If they are unable to attend, ask them to put their thoughts and concerns in a letter that you can bring with you and give to the school.

- **Provide the school with outside evaluations or information.** If you have reports or letters that you will be using to support your position, it's a good idea to give these to the school ahead of time. If you present it for the first time at the meeting, the school may ask to reschedule so they can have a chance to look over the information more carefully.

Making all these preparations for an eligibility meeting can also help you be more confident that you are a valuable member of your child's IEP team.

ALERT

IDEA requires schools to encourage parental participation in the special education process, including making the decision about eligibility. Participate in full, making sure the team knows all about your child and how his disability is impacting him.

Who Will, and Should, Be at the Meeting

When you walk into the room, don't be surprised if it's packed full of people. Although the notice you received about the meeting had all the invited participants listed, you may not know who they are or why they are included. IDEA requires certain people to be at this meeting, including:

- **You, as your child's parent or guardian.** If you are not in attendance, the school needs to have documentation that there have been at least two attempts to provide you with ten-days' notice of a meeting.
- **Your child,** if he's at the age of majority or older or it is otherwise deemed appropriate for him to attend. Adolescents are sometimes given the opportunity to sit in on a meeting, especially once transition planning is begun, as they are active participants in their own education.
- **Your child's regular education teacher.** If your child does not have an assigned teacher or the teacher is unable to attend, a regular education teacher who teaches children of the same age will be asked to be there.
- **A special education teacher.**
- **An administrator** who is able to speak to the resources available in the school district. This is often the school principal, although in some school districts and circumstances the special education director is the designated administrator.
- **The professional (or professionals) who evaluated your child.** The evaluator is present to interpret the result of the testing as it pertains to

your child's education. In some circumstances the school district will ask another, equally qualified evaluator to the meeting if the initial evaluator is unable to attend.

- **Any other people you or the school district invite** that know your child and have information to contribute to the discussion.

Parents also have the right to bring whomever they wish to a meeting, whether it be a relative for support, a case manager from an outside agency, or an educational advocate. If you will be bringing someone else to the meeting, it's common courtesy to let the school know ahead of time.

What to Expect at an Eligibility Meeting

Walking into that room and seeing all the people there can be intimidating to say the least, especially if they all seem to know each other and are chatting before the meeting begins. Don't worry too much about it, though, as the first thing that happens at a meeting is introductions. The attendees around the table will have a chance to say who they are and what their relationship is to your child. If this doesn't happen, speak up and ask that introductions be made.

Typically the IEP coordinator or special education teacher will run the meeting. After introductions are made, she will recap why you're all there (to determine whether your child is eligible for special education services), review the evaluations and assessments that were recommended, and ask each evaluator in turn to summarize his or her testing, findings, and recommendations.

ESSENTIAL

If you have questions during an evaluator's presentation, don't hesitate to ask. An eligibility meeting follows a certain format, but it's not a formal proceeding.

After the relevant school material has been introduced and summarized, it's your turn to speak about your concerns and any material you have brought with you to support eligibility. Make sure to be ready to provide copies to the school if you haven't already, and be prepared to talk about why you think this information is important. Once you have had a chance to speak, there will be a discussion about whether your child can be found eligible for special education services.

How Eligibility Is Determined

There are two crucial eligibility requirements your child has to meet: (a) he has to have a disabling condition that fits into one of the thirteen categories of disabilities defined by IDEA, and (b) his disabling condition has to have an adverse effect on his education. In some cases, eligibility is clear-cut; your child has a disability as defined under IDEA that is undoubtedly affecting his ability to learn in the general education classroom. In other cases it's not that simple.

One of the main reasons why it can be complicated is because even though IDEA clearly defines the criteria for eligibility for special education and related services, it does not provide definitions for the key terms "disabling condition," "adverse effect," or "education." That leaves those terms open to interpretation, and people often have differing interpretations. The debate about what those terms mean can be complex, confusing, and frustrating, but what it often boils down to are a few questions:

1. Into what category of disability does your child's disabling condition fit?
2. What is considered to be a part of a child's education?
3. What does an "adverse effect" look like in real life?

The Category Question

The question about which category of disability your child falls into sometimes comes up because your child's disability matches one of the categories, but it's not as severe as IDEA requires it to be for eligibility purposes. For example, the definitions for deafness and deaf-blindness both include the words "significant" and "severe," so if your child has a mild or moderate hearing or visual impairment, he cannot be found eligible under those categories. That doesn't mean he can't be found eligible at all, though; the definitions of visual and hearing impairment do not include the same strict language.

This can be true of co-occurring conditions as well. Imagine, for example, that your child has ADHD *and* a learning disability, or autism *and* a mood disorder. In both cases, your child could be found eligible for special education in one of two categories, so the question is which category to use. Sometimes a school district will want to use one over the other because of the programs that are available for a child eligible under a specific category. For example, if there is a program for children with emotional disturbances that the school would like your child with autism to attend, there may be a push to have him found eligible under the category of emotional disturbance.

It may seem like it doesn't matter, but your child really should be found eligible for service according to the disabling condition that most significantly affects his education and will continue to impact his learning. In this scenario, it's more likely that autism will be a continuing challenge to his educational success. In the example of the co-occurring conditions of ADHD and a learning disability, being deemed eligible in the specific learning disability category opens up more options for targeted learning interventions.

As you face the category question, keep in mind that the "I" in IEP stands for "individualized." In other words, it is your child's educational needs that will help the IEP team make a decision about the services he needs, not the checkbox on a piece of paper.

The Education and Adverse Effect Questions

The next hurdle you face is the question of what an education is and how you know whether your child's is being adversely affected. To some the definition of education is very narrow—it's the academic content your child is supposed to be learning in school. If that's how education is defined, then defining adverse effect is easy: If your child is not able to keep up with his peers academically because of his disability, the disability is adversely affecting his education.

However, IDEA doesn't say that children with disabilities are entitled to have the same academic experience as nondisabled peers; it says that they should have the same *educational* experience. That opens the door to take a look at what the whole educational experience involves. The questions that are often asked are:

- If a child isn't having trouble academically but his disability interferes with his ability to have the same physical or social-emotional educational experience as other children, is that an "adverse effect?"
- Are social skills and the ability to control emotions part of the educational experience?
- Is learning to perform activities of daily living independently part of a free appropriate public education?

According to court rulings in situations where parents have challenged school districts' answers to those questions, these things *are* all part of the educational experience IDEA is trying to define. In one groundbreaking case (*Mr. I v. Maine School Administrative District No. 55*), the First Circuit Court of Appeals pointed out that IDEA says children with disabilities are entitled to a free and appropriate education that includes the services needed to "meet their unique needs and prepare them for further education, employment, and independent living." (20 U.S.C. § 1400(d)(1)(A))

The point the court was making is that social skills, emotional control, and the ability to be as physically independent as possible are all necessary pieces of being prepared for employment and independent living. Your school district may not agree, but if you think your child's disabling condition is having an adverse effect in those areas, know that there is legal precedent to support you.

What Happens Next?

Luckily, determining whether or not your child has a disabling condition that is adversely affecting her education is typically less complicated and overwhelming than all of that. Most of the time all the members of the IEP team want the same thing—to help your child be successful—and they will work together to find a way to make that happen. If that means defining "adverse effect" as making limited progress or not being able to meet her own academic potential (this may be talked about as the difference between your child's performance scores and ability scores), IDEA gives the team the flexibility to make those decisions at its discretion.

If Your Child Isn't Found Eligible for Special Education Services

Sometimes a team will not be able to come to a consensus that your child is eligible for special education services. You have a few options to explore if this is the outcome of the eligibility meeting: You can agree that the evaluative data doesn't support a need for special education services, you can raise the question as to whether your child may be eligible for services under Section 504, or you can continue to advocate for your child's need for special education services, either by seeking an independent evaluation or asking for mediation under your due process rights.

If Your Child Is Eligible for Services

On the other hand, if the team determines your child is eligible for services and this is a joint eligibility/IEP development meeting, the team will move to the IEP portion of the meeting. It will be time to start talking about what your child's educational needs are and what services are appropriate to meet those needs. If time is running short or you have not planned on having developing an IEP, another meeting will be scheduled to get a plan written within the next thirty days. That time between meetings isn't always a bad thing; you can use it to do everything you can to be your child's best advocate when it's time to talk services.

CHAPTER 14

Being Your Child's Advocate Before the IEP Meeting

You don't have to wait until your child's IEP meeting or until things go wrong to start being an advocate. The best time to start advocating for your child is *before* the meeting. It gives you time to sort through the information you have on hand and to come up with an idea of what you think your child's ideal education plan should look like. As you're working through what is going to be the best plan to help your child learn, think about how the regular education class will fit into that. Undoubtedly you want your child to have the best program in place, but it's important to keep two things in mind: Special education is supposed to make it easier for your child to learn the general education curriculum, and social interaction is part of learning, too.

Creating an Ideal IEP

As you put together the perfect IEP, you don't have to limit yourself to thinking about what the school has available for programs and services. If the school already has a program that fits your child's needs, that's great, but if it doesn't, then you should advocate for what you think is going to be best for your child. The idea is to figure out what her plan would look like in a perfect world in which money, staff, space, or teacher training weren't an issue. It's the end result of all your research, but it's really a place to start from when you're in the IEP meeting.

The best way to start building the perfect plan is by imagining your child in a classroom in which she's happy and learning easily. What does that classroom look like? How many other children are there? Who is teaching the class? Is there a teacher's aide, tutor, or interpreter in the classroom? Are all the kids working on the same thing, or are they working individually or in small groups?

Once you have that picture in your head you can start going through a checklist of the things that need to be part of your child's IEP to make that picture a reality. Here are some things to think about (a blank copy of this IEP Preparation checklist can be found in Appendix C):

What Classroom Setting Is Best?

Think about the type of classroom that is going to be the best match for your child. It's not enough to be able to see it in your head; you need to be able to talk about what makes it perfect. This means thinking about things like whether you think your child needs a few hours of support during the day or if a full-day special education program would be better. Since your child's abilities may not match her age, you'll also want to think about whether she'd do better being around kids hers age or kids on her same level of functioning. Check off all the options that apply and add your notes at the end of the section.

○ Regular education classroom with pull-out special education support
○ Regular education classroom with in-class support
○ Regular education classroom with accommodations
○ Specific type of special education classroom (note the program in your notes)

○ Multiage classroom
○ Classroom with same-age peers

What Are the Needs in Terms of Staffing?

Once you've defined the perfect classroom, start thinking about who is running it, what their training is, and how many kids and teachers there are. What you're doing is coming up with the ideal staffing situation for your child's classroom. If you think he needs to be in a classroom with one teacher for every five students, say so. If you want the teacher to have specific training working with children with learning disabilities (for example), write that down, too.

○ Small teacher-to-student ratio (no more than ____ students per teacher)
○ Classroom aide
○ One-to-one aide
○ Special education teacher trained in teaching your child's specific disability
○ Special education teacher
○ Regular education teacher with special education support available

How Does Your Child Need to Be Taught?

By now you have a pretty good idea of at least some of the ways your child doesn't learn well, if not a good sense of how she does learn well. Use that information to identify what types of teaching strategies and curriculum you would like to see put into place for your child. You may not know what's out there and that's okay. Just write down the ways you know your child learns best.

○ Applied behavioral analysis (ABA)
○ Increased visual supports in teaching (i.e., picture schedules, visual directions)
○ Sign language
○ Braille or large print
○ Specific curriculum or method of teaching (write it down in the notes)

Which Related Services Are Needed?

Remember that related services aren't the way your child is taught. It's the other things that are needed to help your child get the most from his education, like assistive technology or various types of therapies. Suggestions for helpful related services can often be found in the "Recommendations" section of an evaluation report, but there may be some you think are needed that weren't mentioned. Write them down and don't forget to make note of how often per week each service should happen and how long each session should be.

○ Psychological services and/or counseling
○ Social work services
○ Occupational therapy services
○ Physical therapy services
○ Speech-language and audiology services
○ Orientation and mobility services
○ Special transportation
○ Interpreter services
○ Assistive technology
○ School nurse services

Is There an Existing Program That Fits?

Here's a chance to let the school district know that you've done your homework. Identify any existing program—whether it is part of the school district, a private school, or a program in a nearby school district—that would meet your child's educational needs. The district may not agree to place your child in that program, but it will give them a better sense of what type of program you want for your child.

What Goals Need to Be Worked On?

Goals are always one of the harder pieces of an IEP. Your child's IEP should include learning goals based on the areas in which he's having trouble, but according to IDEA, it should also include "functional goals." The school may want to focus more on the academics, but keep in mind that if your child is having difficulty with skills that are not purely academic (life skills or social skills, for example), those should be included, too. You can write things as simple as "Amanda will improve her reading comprehension skills," or as complex as "Amanda will begin to self-regulate her emotions in her interactions with peers, to the point where argumentative behavior and outbursts are occurring only once weekly."

Are There Other Needs to Consider?

Don't forget to think about issues and needs that aren't as visible but also need to be documented. This can be anything from the fact that your child is going to need transportation to his new program to things that don't even seem related to the disability you're talking about. For example, if your child has severe food allergies in addition to learning needs, it's important that you mention that the school staff needs to be trained how and when to use an EpiPen, and classroom accommodations need to be made to make sure he doesn't have contact with foods that could cause a reaction.

- ○ Health issues that involve staff training
- ○ Medication
- ○ Social needs
- ○ Special transportation
- ○ Transition planning
- ○ Life skills/vocational needs
- ○ Percentage of time or number of hours spent in the regular education classroom _____
- ○ Modifications needed
- ○ Accommodations for testing

Supporting Your Ideal IEP

Once you've figured out what you want for your child, the next step in being a successful advocate is supporting what you think is best for your child. Hopefully you and the school will be on the same page, but you need to be prepared for the likelihood that your vision for your child's education won't match the school's vision. Knowing that is important. As you gather what you need to back up your own position, you'll be prepared not only to defend your position but also to say why you don't agree with the school's recommendations.

Learning the school district's position regarding your child's special education program doesn't have to be difficult. If you can't tell from reports and records, it doesn't hurt to simply ask school personnel what they will recommend.

Review the Available Information

Since you've already gone through the evaluation reports and your child's education records in detail to prepare for an eligibility meeting, you already have a pretty good idea of what all the information has to say. The difference is that as you review the information this time, you're not only looking for what it does say but for the things it doesn't say, too. That's not to say you're going to have to scour the paperwork to glean information, just that you may need to read between the lines a little bit.

As you take another look at your child's records—which should include all of the information in your records binder in addition to new reports and work—it's just as important to pay attention to comments made in conversations or notes and written on homework as it is to read the recommendations in evaluation reports.

Looking Through Your Child's Records with a Critical Eye

You may find that your child's teacher made a passing comment in a progress report about her belief that your child would benefit from a certain type of service, or that your child's education records contain correspondence between school personnel that talks about what services they don't think would be helpful to your child. You may even find an item in the newspaper about budget cuts and programs that are affected or a note in the school newsletter about the types of classrooms the school has.

As you find each comment or report that you think will helpful, highlight the portion, comment, or score that is important and set it aside. Once you have everything set aside, grab a sticky note and note to whom the information can be attributed, what his or her relationship is to your child, and what role this person has in the school district. For example, if you are looking at a report card comment made by a teacher your child had in fifth grade, you might write, "Mr. Small, 5th grade regular education teacher, report card dated 10/01/13."

FACT

A pile of papers and sticky notes is hard to sort through and won't look all that professional when you go into a meeting, so you may want to take the time to make a chart of the information. Don't forget to leave a box in which you can note how each piece of information is supportive (or not) of your ideal IEP.

Individually, each of these items isn't all that significant, but put together they make a powerful portfolio of information to support your ideal IEP. And if it doesn't support your position, at least you know you'll need more information to successfully argue your case for certain services. You'll also have a better idea of what the school has in hand to support their recommendations.

Creating a Chart to Support Your Ideal IEP

Take, for example, John, a child who has a known anxiety disorder. He has a 504 plan in place, but despite accommodations, his unfocused and unpredictable behavior continued to interfere with his learning so he was referred for evaluation for special education services. The evaluation revealed that John also has ADHD and recommended further testing to confirm the presence of a learning disability. John's parents drafted their ideal IEP.

They would like John to spend the majority of his time in the regular education classroom with his same-age peers, but go to the resource room for additional instruction in reading and writing—the areas in which he's having the most trouble. They would like to see a support person in the classroom to reduce the teacher-student ratio but do not want that person to be a one-to-one aide for John because they think one of his goals should be to learn how to work more independently. However, they would like to see that support person available to shadow John at lunch, recess, and other transition times. Additionally, John's parents would like the regular education teacher to consult with the special education teacher to come up with a rewards-based behavior management plan to use with John.

As they sorted through John's records, they found information that would support some of their wishes, but also some information that would suggest the school district might not be willing to provide some of the pieces of their plan. Here's what their chart might look like.

▼ **IEP SUPPORTING EVIDENCE CHART**

Document/comment	Who wrote/said it?	Date	What it supports	What it refutes
John's ABC chart showing trouble with peers during transition times.	Regular education teacher	Ongoing	Support person to shadow lunch and recess	Full-time mainstreaming
Evaluation report showing deficits in literacy skills	Evaluator	10/01/13	Resource room instruction	n/a
Article in paper about support staff being laid off due to budget cuts	The *Times*	9/28/13	n/a	Support staff added to classroom
Suspension report comments re: "placement may need to be rethought."	Principal	9/15/13	n/a	Regular education classroom placement

Keeping Track of How Your Child Is Doing

Don't forget to keep adding information right up until the day of the IEP meeting. Your child will continue going to school and is in the same educational program in which he's been having trouble. That's not likely to stop just because he was evaluated and found eligible for special education. In fact, if he did stop having difficulties, he probably doesn't need special education! If you are not already saving samples of his work, start doing so now and don't forget to update your communication log every time you have a conversation with someone about your child and school.

Finding Out about Your Child's Educational Program Options

It's not enough to just know what the ideal program for your child would look like. The reality is that unless you have found a specific program in the district that is perfect for your child, you'll have to be ready to talk with the IEP team about how to modify your child's current program. That may mean talking about the types of programs and placements that are available. Many school districts, for example, have some sort of specialized classroom for children with moderate to severe intellectual disabilities, or a program for kids with behavioral issues. Or it may mean finding creative ways to make use of the resources available to modify your child's program to meet her needs.

Regardless, you need to know what your child's current program looks like, what else is available, and understand the concept of what IDEA calls the *least restrictive environment* (LRE).

What's the Current Program?

Your child's program isn't just the classroom she's in; it's also the way she's being taught, the classes and subjects she's taking, and any related services she has in place. Her program is the overall education experience. Her *placement* is the classroom or types of classrooms in which she will be taught. For instance, your child might have placement in the regular education classroom, but her program includes a tutor, speech therapy services, and accommodations in the classroom.

ALERT

Talking about programs can be confusing to parents because the word is used not only to describe your child's entire educational experience but also to describe specific types of special education classrooms. If you're unsure which is being discussed, speak up and ask.

Before an initial IEP meeting, it's fairly likely that your child's program consists of the regular education classroom, any informal accommodations being made (or those made through a 504 plan), and maybe some specialized instruction provided by a response-to-intervention plan. For now, that's your child's current program.

Understanding Least Restrictive Environment (LRE)

When you start looking at making placement and program changes, IDEA requires that every child be placed in the least restrictive environment in which his or her educational needs can be met. IDEA says two things about LRE that are important to understand when you and the school start talking about your child's program:

1. Your child with a disability should be educated alongside children without disabilities to the "maximum extent that is appropriate."
2. Your child with a disability should only be placed in special classes, separate schools, or removed from the regular education class if the disability is so severe that supplementary aids and services are not enough to make sure your child is getting an appropriate education.

Like many things in IDEA, this leaves the interpretation open for debate. The intent is to make sure that children with disabilities are included in the regular education classroom as often as possible and are able to go to school as close to their home as possible.

Some school districts interpret this to mean that before a child is placed in a classroom specifically for children with disabilities, the school needs to try all other options of educating a child within the regular education classroom with as little support as possible. So, you may hear that providing a one-to-one aide for your child in the regular education classroom is more restrictive than providing him with some time in the resource room, but it's less restrictive than placing him a special education classroom for children with intellectual disabilities.

What is often lost in the conversation about least restrictive environment is that there isn't one set LRE that will fit the needs of all children with disabilities. The intent is to make sure every child is placed in his or her own least restrictive environment, which is the placement in which a child is going to learn best based on his or her individual needs. In some cases the least restrictive environment will be in the regular education classroom with support, but in others the least restrictive environment is a special education classroom or program with specific teaching methods.

For instance, the least restrictive environment for a child with a mild hearing impairment is most likely in the regular education classroom with supports like an auditory trainer, an interpreter, and/or speech therapy services. On the other hand, the least restrictive environment in which a child with complete hearing loss and limited language skills could learn might be in special program for deaf children, even if that program is not in her local school district.

ESSENTIAL

The LRE argument can be used in either direction. You can argue that your child should be given a chance in the mainstream classroom before being placed in a special program, but you can also argue that your child's needs are so severe that he will only be able to learn in a special program.

What Types of Programs Are There?

The IEP team has the leeway to create whatever type of program they think is going to be effective for your child, but there are some common placement options to look at. They include:

- **Placement in the regular education classroom with support services.** These support services can vary. They may include a tutor or aide to work directly with your child, assistive technology, related services, different types of instruction or materials, or any combination of these things.
- **Split placement in the regular education and special education classrooms.** This is a very common way to set up programs for children who do not have severe disabilities. The team determines how much time per day of specialized—individual or small-group—instruction your child needs. He spends that learning time in a resource room and the rest of his day in the regular classroom. The resource room

will typically have kids coming in and out throughout the day to meet their individual educational needs, too.

- **Placement in a special education classroom specific to your child's needs.** If your child is unable to learn in the regular classroom and there is a program with specialized instruction for kids with similar disabilities, this can be a consideration. Often there are classes for children with autism, emotional disturbances, significant learning disabilities, communication issues, or significant intellectual disabilities.
- **Placement in a specialized program outside of your school district.** This would include things like private schools, residential programs, and hospital programs.

Evaluating Your District's Programs

All of the placement and program options can be a little overwhelming, which is why it's a good idea to see if you can get a sense of what type of program the school is going to recommend for your child. That doesn't mean you shouldn't find out about all the available programs, though. Contact your school district's special education department to ask about what programs and placements there are for children who have similar educational needs to those of your child. You may find that people are hesitant to provide you with the information and will tell you things like, "We're not ready to discuss programs for your child; that's a decision to be made by the IEP team."

Don't let that stop you finding out more information. Make it clear that you are not shopping for a program for your child and that you just want to be informed about what's available so you can be an equal participant in that IEP meeting. Try saying something along the lines of, "I understand that the IEP has to work together regarding placement, but in order to make sure I'm an informed member of the team I think it would be very helpful to know more about the programs in the district. Is there another reason I shouldn't be gathering this information?"

Start Visiting Programs

Once you have an idea of what programs are available, it would be very beneficial for you to be able to visit them before the IEP meeting. Be prepared to put your request in writing and to be persistent in letting people know that you don't think you'd be able to support the IEP team's recommendation without having some firsthand knowledge of the different placements.

Putting your request in writing will strengthen your case, as it documents your request and will most likely create a written response that will also be part of your child's records. If you get a verbal response instead of a written one, make sure to write a follow-up letter acknowledging what was agreed to in the conversation. There is a sample Request to Visit Programs letter in Appendix B.

When to Visit and Who Should Come with You

What you are trying to observe when you visit a program is how it works on an ordinary day. Having someone new or unfamiliar in the classroom can throw off the teacher as well as disrupt the students' routine, too, so the fewer people who visit, the more likely you are to get an accurate picture of the program structure. It's best if you stick to the parents or guardians who are familiar with your child and will be part of the decision-making process at the IEP meeting.

Try to arrange enough time to see the program from the moment students arrive at school all the way through lunchtime or from lunchtime to the end of the day. That way you're able to see how transitions are handled as well as some teaching time. You'll also want to make sure you schedule visits as far out from the IEP meeting as possible—that way you have time to revisit a program if you need to and to get in touch with the teacher to ask any questions that may have come up during your visit.

What Not to Do

Asking questions during your visit is only appropriate if you have someone from the school district accompanying you. Otherwise, you'll be interrupting the educational process by taking the teacher's attention away from the students. That's not fair to the teacher and students, and it also will prevent you from seeing the environment as it is on any other day.

It's also not appropriate to ask questions about the students in the classroom. Although it may be tempting (and informative) to ask, "Who is that child and what disability does he have?" the same rights that protect your child's privacy in school apply to other kids as well. You can, however, let the administrator know you'd be interested in speaking with some of the parents of children in the program and provide your contact information to pass along.

Questions to Ask

When you do have an opportunity to sit down and speak with the teacher or program director, there are some basic questions that you can ask to get more information about the classroom and whether it seems like a good match for your child. There is a more detailed Program Visitation checklist for your use in Appendix C, but some of the questions you should ask include:

- What is the basic demographic of the students in the classroom? (This includes information about things such as the age range, type of disabilities, and grade levels at which students are working.)
- How many staff people are there and what are their roles and credentials?
- What type of teaching is used in the program? (This means not only curriculum but also whether students are taught in small groups or individually.)
- What behavior management plan(s) are in place?
- Do students spend time with regular education classrooms?
- Are students pulled out for related services or are they integrated into the classroom?

If you're not able to get all the research done before the IEP meeting, don't panic. Do what you can and go to the IEP meeting armed with the information you do have. If there are things that come up at the meeting that you are unsure about or need to research further, you are not obligated to make any decisions right at the table.

CHAPTER 15

All about IEPs (Individualized Education Program)

The acronym IEP is used in so many different ways that once you get to the point of creating one for your child, you may not know how the phrase is being used anymore. You'll often hear the meeting at which the plan is being written referred to as "the IEP," without the word "meeting" on the end. More often (and more accurately), IEP is used to talk about the written plan of what your child's special education program looks like.

What Is an IEP?

Every child who receives special education services has an IEP, or an individualized education program. It is the written document that serves as the blueprint for your child's special education program. It has information about your child's placement, her strengths and weaknesses, her related services, her goals, and her behavior plan if she has one. While the form may look the same for every child, the information on the form should look very different—that's why the "I" in IEP stands for individualized.

Once all the information has been agreed upon and you sign the plan giving permission for the program and services, it becomes a legally binding document. That means the school district is now required by law to provide all the services and accommodations included in the plan, and it must work toward helping your child achieve her goals. The school is not, however, required by law to make sure your child meets her goals in a specific time frame. Her IEP will be reviewed yearly to see what progress has been made and whether the goals need to be adjusted or changed.

Who Are the Members of the IEP Team?

You may think you met all the members of the IEP team at your child's eligibility meeting, but once your child has been found eligible for special education services, the people who sit around the table change a little bit. For the initial IEP meeting—the one at which you are creating your child's first special education plan—you're most likely going to see some of the same faces you saw at the eligibility meeting. Your child's regular education teacher will be there, the evaluator will probably be there, and a school administrator will be there, too. What may be different this time around is that instead of just any special education teacher in the school, you're much more likely to see the specific teacher who will be working with your child. That's helpful if you have questions about how the special education program for your child will work.

You may also see the specialists—like speech therapists or physical therapists—who might be working with your child, but technically they can only attend to answer general questions about their services. Until the team talks about services for your child and a plan is executed, specialists are not official members of the IEP team. Once your child has an IEP in place, anyone who is working with her to meet her goals becomes a member of the IEP team and can (and should!) attend future meetings. In addition to all of these other people, you are a key member of the IEP team, too.

Know Your IEP Rights

Being a member of your child's IEP team isn't a privilege; it's your right. In fact, it's one of the most important rights given to you under IDEA. Although you may feel that what you have to say isn't as important as the professionals around the table, that's far from the truth. As your child's parent and best advocate, you are able to provide critical information about development, social and family history, abilities and difficulties outside of school, and how school has gone for her up until now. IDEA recognizes that your input is a crucial part of making sure your child's team puts together the best plan for her needs.

The right to participate equally isn't the only right you have when it comes to IEPs and special education. You already know you have the right to ask that your child be evaluated for special education, the right to ask for and review your child's education records, and the right to ask that corrections be made to those education records if necessary.

You can do this by sending a letter to the school district, noting what you think is incorrect and explaining how you would like to see the record amended. There's a Request to Modify or Change Educational Records letter in Appendix B, but here's how that letter might read:

Dear Ms. Special Education Administrator,

Recently, I received and reviewed a copy of my child's education records. I know that under IDEA I have the right to request amendment to any inaccurate or misleading information or information that violates my child's privacy. I would like to exercise that right and request the following portions or files be amended, for the following reasons:

The suspension report dated October 1, 2014 does not accurately reflect what happened in the classroom. If you look at the teacher's notes dated the same day, you will note that my child was provoked by another child and was not the instigator as noted on the suspension form. This report is misleading and I request that the information be corrected.

As stated, I believe the information above to be inaccurate, misleading, or a violation of Sally's privacy, and I request that the education record be changed immediately to fix this situation.

I look forward to seeing your written decision on this matter. Thank you.

Respectfully,
Ima Y.

Prior Written Notice

You also have the right to be informed in writing about any action or changes the school district proposes to make in regard to your child. This is known as prior written notice. It is the written communication that tells you about what the school wants or is refusing to do in regard to your child's education.

ESSENTIAL

Sometimes you will be told about a meeting or proposed action by phone call or in person. You still have the right to a prior written notice. Make sure you ask that the school gives you one so that you have all the information in writing.

Prior written notice is a way of making sure you're kept in the loop and that both you and the school can prove it. Although that may sound somewhat ominous, that isn't always the case. Sometimes it is just a way to give you enough time to know that a meeting is planned and the reasons why the meeting is being held. By law, prior written notice must include:

- A description of what action is being proposed or refused
- The reasons why the school is proposing or denying the action

- All the other options considered by the school and why those options weren't found to be acceptable
- A description of every piece of data used to support the proposed or refused action, including evaluations, records, reports, etc.
- Any other information that plays an important role in this decision

The prior written notice for an IEP meeting will look very different than the one sent to you about other matters, but they must be sent to you in all cases. You have the right to receive prior written notice whenever the school proposes to initiate or change the identification or educational placement of your child. You should also get a notice when the school wants to change the way your child's FAPE is provided, make changes to your child's eligibility status, or further evaluate your child. If you do not receive prior written notice in any of these situations, it's easy enough to request one. All you have to do is write a letter to ask for the notice. For your convenience, a sample letter is provided in Appendix B.

Signing the IEP

One thing that parents don't always know is that you also have the right to disagree with what the IEP the team suggests for your child. In a perfect situation, everyone sitting around the table at an IEP meeting will agree on all the goals, all the services, and everything else your child needs. That happens more often than you may think, but it doesn't always happen. And when it doesn't happen, it can be very easy to feel intimidated and think, "Well, these people are the professionals so they must know what's best for my child," or "It doesn't matter what I say; they're not going to be willing to listen to me." As an equal member of your child's IEP team, your opinion matters. As your child's parent, your signature matters even more.

This cannot be stressed enough: *If you do not agree with the proposed individualized education program, you do not have to sign it and give your permission for it to be put into place.* No matter what anybody tells you, you don't have to sign. If you don't sign, the school cannot change your child's educational program without taking it to mediation and a hearing. Taking those legal steps, however, is not the first way to approach disagreements.

Requesting Changes to the IEP

You can request changes be made to the IEP at any time, whether you've signed it or not. At that first meeting, though, it's better to talk about what you don't agree with before you sign any forms. Be prepared not only to talk about what you do not agree with but also to tell the team members why you don't agree and what you would like to have happen instead. When it's something simple, like changing the amount of time per week your child receives a related service, it's easy enough to just have a discussion about it. Something bigger, like disagreeing with the entire program or asking that your child be placed in a different classroom than the school is suggesting, will not necessarily be a simple discussion.

There needs to be evidential support that the program developed for your child is the right one for her. This is true whether it's you making the request or the school making the suggestion. If you do not agree with the rest of the team or that the evidence on which they are basing a decision is valid, you'll need to have documentation to back up what you want. That's when you might want to consider having an independent educational evaluation done.

The Right to an Independent Evaluation

The right to an independent evaluation is another right provided to you under IDEA. If you do not agree with the results of the evaluation the school district conducts of your child, you have the right to have her evaluated by a professional who is not employed by or associated with the school department. IDEA says that the results of an independent evaluation have to be considered when making a decision about your child's education. It also says you have the right to ask that the evaluation is provided at public expense, meaning the school district pays for it. Here are some common reasons you might ask for an independent evaluation:

- You think your child has a disability, but the school's evaluation didn't find evidence of one.
- The school's evaluation says your child has a disability, but you don't agree or you disagree with which disability your child has been identified as having.

- The school evaluation didn't look at all the areas you think it should have, or you think the results are inaccurate.
- You don't agree with the placement suggested or goals that are being written based on the evaluation results.
- You and the school disagree on your child's least restrictive environment and you would like another opinion before making a final decision.

What's an Independent Evaluation?

When you request an independent evaluation, IDEA says the school district must give you information about where you can get that evaluation done. If you are asking that it be provided at public expense, the evaluation must follow the same criteria as the one the school already had done. That means the credentials of the evaluator have to be comparable, the location has to be comparable, and the testing itself has to be comparable. Unlike a school evaluation, though, there are no timelines to follow. Of course, if this evaluation is holding up the process of putting special education services into place for your child, you're going to want to have it done as soon as possible. That's not always soon if you are asking the school to pay for the evaluation.

Who Pays for an Independent Evaluation?

IDEA says that parents have the right to ask for an independent evaluation at public expense, but it also says the school district has a couple of options when a parent makes this request. The school district can agree to pay for an evaluation or file a due process complaint for a hearing to prove that the school's evaluation is appropriate. If the hearing officer finds that the evaluation was appropriate, you can still have an independent evaluation done, but the school doesn't have to pay for it. Sometimes a hearing officer will ask for another evaluation as part of the hearing process. In that case. the evaluation is always done at public expense.

If you are requesting an independent educational evaluation and want it to be at public expense, you must put that request in writing. There is a sample letter in Appendix B that you can use to make this request. The school district has the right to ask you why you want an independent evaluation, but you are not obligated to provide your reasons. IDEA specifically says that your school district can't hold up paying for an evaluation or filing for due process if you don't provide a reason for wanting a different evaluation.

Tips for Finding an Evaluator

The school has to give you information about where you can get an independent evaluation done, but you don't have to use that information to find someone to evaluate your child. You can find a qualified evaluator on your own, provide the criteria for evaluation, and set it up yourself.

ALERT

Avoid using the yellow pages to find an independent evaluator. Being listed in the phone book is not a substitution for a good word-of-mouth reputation.

There are a number of ways to find someone to evaluate your child. You can start by checking with your child's pediatrician and asking for a referral to a specialist. You can also:

- Speak to parents of children with the same type of disability as your child, and ask whom they would recommend.
- Call your local disability rights center or parent advocacy group and ask for a list of evaluators.
- Visit or speak with your state's Parent Training and Information Center. The Department of Education's Office of Special Education Programs funds these centers and there is at least one in each state. You can find the one in your state at the Parent Technical Assistance Center Network's website.
- Call a local or national organization that specializes in working with families and children who are affected by the type of disability your child has.
- Check with local hospitals and nearby universities to see if they have an evaluator on staff.

Once you have a list of names to work with, you can start making phone calls to ask potential evaluators about their credentials, experience, cost, availability (both for testing and for attending an IEP meeting), and whether or not the evaluator has worked with or for your child's school district in the past. While you're speaking, you should be able to get a pretty good sense of whether or not this is somebody you'd be comfortable talking to about your concerns and your child.

QUESTION

Does it matter if an independent evaluator has contracted with my child's school district?
An evaluator who has been paid for work done for your child's school may not be as impartial as an evaluator who has no association with the district. It's a good idea to ask up front about the evaluator's relationship with the school district and make a decision from there.

Talking to an Evaluator

It's not enough just to choose someone to do an independent evaluation. If you are pursuing another evaluation, it's because you and the school don't agree on some important issues. This evaluation is your chance to have a professional help you make your case. When you talk to the evaluator, be honest about what you are looking for and explain your disagreement with the school as calmly as possible. The more reasonable and articulate you are, the more likely the evaluator is going to hear your concerns.

Let the evaluator know what you are hoping to see in the test results and ask to see a draft of the report before it is finalized. If the draft doesn't have very specific recommendations about what type of instruction and services would benefit your child, ask the evaluator to include them. Be aware, though, that a reputable evaluator will not make recommendations that the data doesn't support. It is possible that this evaluation will support the school's position, not yours.

Whatever the findings, make sure you are prepared to discuss them in detail at your child's IEP meeting, hopefully with the evaluator at your side.

That way the evaluator can help you use that information as you and the team start writing your child's IEP.

An In-Depth Look at an IEP

IDEA says that certain information has to be in every child's IEP, but there isn't one form or format that every state has to use. Most states have developed forms that school districts can use as is or as a starting point for an IEP in order to make sure that all the required information is in your child's plan.

ESSENTIAL

Using a form to write an IEP can make it harder to be flexible in including factors that may not be on the form but are important to your child's education. Keep in mind that you can always ask the team to include a separate page of information or notes as part of your child's IEP.

According to IDEA, an IEP has to have basic demographic information about your child and identify the disability under which he is eligible for special education services. It also has to have a long list of other things included as well.

Present Level of Performance (PLOP)

This is how the IEP begins. It's a statement that talks about your child's current level of academic and functional performance. The PLOP talks about how your child's level of performance compares to the general education classroom expectations for his grade level and how his disability affects that performance. In this case, *academics* means the subjects your child studies in school (reading, writing, math, history, science, etc.) and the skills he is expected to master in each subject area. The question that needs to be answered in the PLOP in terms of academics is: Where is your child academically *right now* and how does his disability affect his ability to be involved and make progress in the regular education curriculum?

Functional performance is different. IDEA does not provide specific examples of functional skills, but in legal comments about IDEA the U.S.

Department of Education clarified that functional performance refers to "skills or activities that are not considered academic or related to a child's academic achievement" and are part of your child's everyday life and routine (§71 Fed. Reg. at 46661). Some of the functional skills that the IEP teams might consider talking about in your child's PLOP statement include:

- **Social and behavior skills.** How your child's disability impacts his ability to make friends, communicate appropriately with others, and understand the social rules and cues around him.
- **Basic life skills.** How your child's disability affects his ability to do things for himself like get dressed, eat, and go to the bathroom.
- **Mobility skills.** How your child's disability impacts his ability to get around physically.

When all of this information is put together, the IEP can write a present-levels-of-performance statement that talks in detail about how your child's disability affects his ability to learn and to do the daily things that are necessary to participate in the general education classroom.

Annual Goals

Your child's PLOP will provide information about her areas of weakness and her needs based on her disability. Using that, the IEP team can develop a set of goals your child works toward in order to make progress toward meeting the grade-level expectations.

It's really important that all the team members remember that it's not reasonable to expect your child will "catch up." In fact, that idea defeats the purpose of having goals. The *overall* goal is to help your child move forward in her education by addressing the things that stand in the way of her learning. Your child's annual goals should be measurable, meaning it should be easy to see if she's making progress toward meeting each goal.

Explanation of How Progress Will Be Measured and Reported

This section of the IEP explains how your child's progress toward goals will be measured, something that's often referred to as *evaluation criteria*. Basically what that means is the IEP team has to decide how your child's progress will be measured, when it will be measured, and how well your child has to do in order for the team to consider the goal met. The way it's measured doesn't have to be complicated—it can even be through school-work, quizzes, or observation—but it does have to be documented. It also has to be done the way it's written in the IEP and in the time frame the team decides upon.

IDEA also requires that the school keep parents up-to-date on progress. That way if progress isn't being made, a meeting can be called to talk about whether the goals or your child's program need to be changed.

ALERT

A school is only required to report progress as often as it reports progress on children not in special education, which means you'll probably be updated when report cards or progress reports come out. If you want more frequent updates, talk to your child's teacher about how that can happen.

Special Education

Your child's IEP must explain what specialized instruction he will receive to meet the needs outlined in his IEP. Remember, special education is the way your child will be taught differently than his peers to make sure he's learning the same things they are. That means the special education services section should only talk about the areas in which he needs support because of his disability. It's a place to talk about the different types of instruction, accommodations, and modifications your child will need as support to meet his goals. If he's only going to need two hours of one-to-one reading instruction in the resource room, this is where that's stated. If he needs to be in a full-time special education classroom to learn, then that's what this section will say.

Related Services

It depends on your school district's form as to whether or not related services and special education services are two separate sections, but they are often tied together. Related services are the types of services your child will need to help him get the most out of his special education program. The special education services for a child who has a severe hearing impairment, for example, may be in a special classroom for children with hearing impairments. However, he will also need speech therapy to help meet goals around improving language and communication. This is a related service.

The section about related services should not only explain what the service is but also what goals and skills it will help your child attain, as well as detail how often and for how long the service will happen. For instance, it may say "speech therapy twice weekly for an hour each session."

Supplementary Aids and Services

IDEA doesn't clearly define what types of things fit into this category, and what it does say doesn't really help shed much light on it. IDEA says this is "aids, services, and other supports that are provided in regular education classes, other education-related settings, and in extracurricular and nonacademic settings, to enable children with disabilities to be educated with non-disabled children to the maximum extent appropriate." (IDEA, Sec. 300.42)

That leaves a lot of room for interpretation, which can actually work to your child's advantage. While the school district might argue that supplementary aids and services only include assistive technology or special equipment your child might need, that argument fails to consider the "services" part of the statement. If you look at it from a service perspective, this section could include:

- Support staff like a one-to-one aide, a tutor, a behavioral consultant, or someone to assist with physical needs.
- Changes to your child's physical environment, like a seating chart for the bus or lunchroom or the furniture being arranged in a certain way in your child's classroom. (This might happen in the case of a physical disability that makes it difficult for your child to get around without support, for example, if your child's impaired vision requires the room to be set up a certain way.)
- The staff or equipment needed to make sure your child has information presented in a format that allows her to learn—for instance, recorded instructions, lecture notes, or visual directions.

Modifications and Accommodations for Testing

All states are now required to measure all students' achievement, and that's usually done with standardized testing. This section provides the school with a place to list the types of accommodations your child will need to participate in that testing. This can be anything from having extra time to complete the test to having a quieter space in which to work to being able to take the test verbally instead of in written form.

Statement of Nonparticipation

This is sometimes done backward—as a statement of participation in the regular education classroom. Either way, this section of the IEP needs to explain how much time your child will spend in the regular education classroom and the special education classroom. It should also explain why the team thought it was best to have your child spend time in a special education setting. This is related to making sure your child's plan reflects her least restrictive environment.

Transition Planning and Statement of Student Rights

Each of these sections comes into play when your child is older. Once your child is between fourteen and sixteen years old, his IEP must include a plan of how his education is preparing him for life when he is done with school. That's a transition plan. Also, starting the year before he reaches the "age of majority," the IEP team must let your child know what his rights regarding special education will be when he reaches that age. If your child will graduate before reaching the age of majority in your state, he must be included in transition planning beginning the year he is sixteen.

FACT

The age of majority is not eighteen years old in all states. It varies between the ages of eighteen and twenty-one.

The Standards-Based IEP

Once you have an understanding of what information an IEP contains, understanding a standards-based IEP isn't all that difficult. A standards-based IEP has all of the same information as any other IEP, but it is written so that it is aligned with your state's educational standards for all students. The No Child Left Behind Act requires states to set standards, or expectations, of what students at each grade level are supposed to know or be able to do in every subject. Because those expectations are already clearly defined, some states have decided that using those standards as a baseline for performance for special education students makes sense.

Using state standards can help to provide more meaningful and measureable goals for your child. With a standards-based IEP, your child's PLOP explains how her current level of performance relates to the state expectations for a student at her grade level. It provides a built-in way to monitor progress (taking the same tests as the rest of the students), and since state standards are often broken into the skills needed to meet a goal, the IEP team can clearly define the skills and knowledge your child needs to gain.

CHAPTER 16

It's All about the Goals

All the hard work you put in to make sure your child gets evaluated and all the wrangling to get services comes down to finding ways to meet your child's goals. Goals are the bottom line of your child's education; they're the targets you're aiming toward for your child academically, socially, and developmentally.

What Is a Goal, Anyway?

An IEP must have annual, measureable goals. That means what the team thinks your child will be able to accomplish is mapped out only one year at a time.

ESSENTIAL

An IEP year isn't exactly the same as a calendar year. It runs from the date the IEP is written to the same date a year later. That means your child's goals may be interrupted by summer vacation or carry over from one grade to the next before the "year" is up.

If you imagine your child's education as a yearlong trip that starts from where he is right now, the goals help show him where he will be at the end of the year. They are the landmarks along the way that his team has decided are important for him to visit on his trip. Goals answer the questions: *Where is your child going this year? What route will he take to get there? Who will be accompanying him on his trip as the navigator?* and *When do we expect him to arrive?*

In real life that means that the IEP team will look at the academic and functional areas in which your child is having trouble as a result of his disability and write statements about how those areas of need will be addressed. It's important to know that IDEA specifically uses the word "functional" in addition to "academic," as some schools aren't always willing to make functional goals a part of an IEP. It's also important to know what goals *aren't*.

Goals are not the Common Core State Standards or other written expectations that your state has in place for all students to meet. Goals are uniquely tied to your child's needs and abilities, so they are personalized. A well-written goal should talk about what your child is able to do now and provide a reasonable expectation of what he'll be able to do by the end of the year with extra help. The key is in the word "reasonable." If it's not reasonable to expect your child to meet the standard for his grade level by the end of the year, then that should not be what the goal states.

Goals are also not set in stone, and the school is not legally obligated to make sure your child meets his goals. They are legally obligated to carry out his IEP and help him work toward his goals, but it's not reasonable to expect that anyone can guarantee he will meet them. That's actually a good thing. Without the pressure of absolutely having to deliver specific results by a certain deadline, both your child and his teachers can concentrate on helping him move forward academically and functionally. Goals are a way to measure whether that movement is happening.

Objectives versus Benchmarks

As you start talking about goals, you may hear a lot about objectives and benchmarks. Special education law used to require that each large goal be broken down into smaller steps to help measure your child's progress. Those small steps were known as objectives, defined as the short-term goals or accomplishments that built up to the bigger goal. So on your child's road trip, the goal would be one of the faraway places he was aiming to get to, and the objective would be the places he knew he was going to pass or stop at along the way.

In the late 1990s, the word *objective* was replaced by the word *benchmark* in special education, but the meaning didn't change. With the reauthorization of IDEA in 2004, schools were no longer required to provide benchmarks for each goal. Now your child's IEP is only required to have "measureable, annual goals" that are designed to meet his needs.

But that doesn't mean schools don't still use objectives or benchmarks—they just don't have to. Annual, measureable goals leave room for the IEP team to write both long-term and short-term goals. It's not unlikely that you will hear someone call those short-term goals "objectives" or "benchmarks."

How Goals and PLOP Go Together

IDEA talks about creating "academic and functional" goals for your child. If you remember, those are the same words that are used to describe your child's present level of performance. That's not a coincidence. In using the same wording in both areas, IDEA is saying that your child's goals should be closely related to his present level of performance. If the PLOP has clearly stated what your child is doing academically and functionally and where that places him in relation to the expectations for his grade level, then his goals should be about how to help him travel between the two.

Making the connection between the PLOP and your child's goals is the first step. The next step is using the PLOP to answer the questions:

- What is your child able to do, and in what skill areas?
- What goal in each skill area will be challenging, but also reachable, for your child in the next year?
- How will we know that your child has made it to this goal?

ALERT

When the team is setting goals for your child, if you discover that the present level of performance is not specific enough to help create goals, then you might want to ask about revisiting the PLOP.

It's possible that your child has many needs in many skill areas, in which case it can be overwhelming to think about all the goals that he might have to work on. Having too many goals can place unrealistic expectations on both your child and his teachers. Instead of having many very specific goals for each subject or functional area, this may be a situation in which creating one goal for each important area of concern is the best way to help your child learn successfully.

The Basics of an Effective Goal

An effective and well-written goal shouldn't leave anything open for interpretation. It should be positively phrased—using words and phrases like "will be able to" instead of "will not"—and talk about a specific skill that can be observed and measured. Saying "John will not be rude to his classmates" is not an effective goal. It doesn't address what John will do instead, and leaves "rude" open to interpretation. There's no way that someone who does not know John would be able to read that goal and understand how to help him. On the other hand, saying "John will use a coping skill [see attached behavior plan] 2 out of every 3 times when dealing with frustrating peer interactions in the classroom" is much more effective. Anyone who reads that goal is able to find the strategies that John should be using and observe whether he is using them two-thirds of the time when his classmates are irritating him. Effective goals can almost be plugged into a formula of:

- *Who* will do *what*
- *How* and *where* they will do it
- *When* (or by when)

Breaking down John's goal, you can see that most of the pieces of the formula are in place.

John (*who*) will use a coping skill (*what*) [see attached behavior plan] (*how*) 2 out of every 3 times (*when*) when dealing with frustrating peer interactions in the classroom (*where*).

What is missing from this goal is "by when." It is also not completely measurable.

A Goal Has to Be Measurable

IDEA says that annual goals have to be measurable. That means that there needs to be a way to see whether or not your child has met or made progress toward her goal. The way it is measured has to be objective, meaning everybody or anybody who looks at it will see it the same way. John's goal to "not be rude" isn't measureable. There is no rude-o-meter, no test for rudeness, and no real way to keep track of how John is not doing something.

Many school districts are moving toward using what special education advocates Peter and Pamela Wright of Wrightslaw.com call SMART IEP goals. SMART stands for:

- **Specific.** Gives a clear description of the skill and knowledge that your child will be working toward learning.
- **Measurable.** Provides a specific way of knowing when progress has been made.
- **Actionable.** Uses action-word language to describe what needs to happen, in what skill area, and at what level.
- **Realistic and relevant.** Bases goals on your child's abilities and present level of performance.
- **Time limited.** Gives a time frame in which the goal will be achieved.

A measurable goal includes either a *performance indicator* or a *rate*. A performance indicator is simply the tool that will be used to measure your child's progress. It's usually a standard test that is given to all children to see how they're doing in a particular subject area. An example of a goal with a performance indicator is:

> *John is currently reading at mid-fifth-grade level as measured by the Scholastic Reading Inventory (SRI). By the end of the fourth quarter of sixth grade, John will be reading at sixth grade entry level, as measured by the SRI.*

That goal is clearly measurable—it even has the words "as measured by" right in it to let people know the way to measure progress is included. The performance indicator is the SRI, a reading test that is given to all the students in the school. John's goal not only indicates where his performance level is now and how the team knows that, but it also provides a reasonable, time-limited, specific goal with the same performance indicator being used to measures his progress as the one that determined his present level of performance. That way, it will be absolutely clear to everybody whether or not John has made progress. Also important to note is that this goal is not unreachable. John is reading considerably below his grade level. The goal does not expect he will catch up to his classmates; it expects that he will continue to make progress at his own pace.

Using a rate to measure a goal is different than using a performance indicator. A rate measures a goal by how many times or at what percentage something is seen. For example:

> *Currently during large-group instruction, John is not waiting for teacher recognition before entering discussion. By January, John will be able to raise his hand three out of five times (60 percent) in order to participate in discussion in three out of four consecutive group instruction sessions, as measured by teacher observation and recordkeeping.*

That's a complicated goal, but it's specific, measurable, actionable, realistic, and time limited. It explains where John's level of performance is right now and how that looks. The goal also explains the progress the IEP team would like to see as a rate (three out of five times), how often it should happen (three out of four lessons per day), by when (January), and how it will be measured. Note that the teacher just thinking John is meeting his goal is not enough; she also needs to have records to prove it.

FACT

A goal doesn't always need to be time limited or have a completion date. Some goals, especially social, behavioral, and daily functioning skill goals, are ongoing and will be carried over from year to year.

A Goal Should Be Assigned to a Specific Team Member

Until your child's IEP is complete, neither is her team. That's because instead of writing goals based on the types of providers available, the types of providers are chosen based on the goals. Each goal on your child's IEP will be assigned to at least one team member. That person is responsible for carrying out the goal and keeping track of progress. But that doesn't mean everyone will work with your child on one goal and never work together. In fact, the majority of your child's goals will probably be a team effort.

For instance, language and communication goals may be primarily the responsibility of the speech therapist, because it's her area of expertise, but she and the classroom teacher will need to work together to make sure your child is able to communicate in the classroom as well. Your child's mobility goals may be the main responsibility of a physical therapist, but the classroom teacher, special education teacher, and physical education teacher will need to make accommodations and modifications to help your child, too.

Why You Should Draft Goals Before a Meeting

Technically, goals are supposed to be written at the IEP meeting, but it's a good idea to have some written up ahead of time. After reading the evaluation reports and speaking with the professionals, you have a good sense of what the tests identify as your child's strengths and weaknesses. Combine that with the knowledge you have from years of raising her and you have a very good idea of what she needs to be working on.

It's unlikely you'll be the only one bringing goals to the table. Although the IEP team is supposed to make all the decisions together, that doesn't mean the school can't write goals ahead of time; it just means they cannot insist that you have to accept their goals without discussion. The fact of the matter is that you only have a limited amount of time for your IEP meeting, so coming to the table with some ideas of what the goals should be is not unusual.

ALERT

If you anticipate the school will have goals prewritten, ask them to provide you with a copy before the meeting. That way you'll have had a chance to review, revise, and ask any questions you might have about them.

It's up to you whether you want to provide the school with a copy of your goals before the meeting or save them for the IEP meeting. The questions you need to consider are: *Will the school district try to find ways to argue against your goals if they have them in advance?* and *Will they ask for more time to review them and postpone the meeting if they don't have them in advance?*

Five Resources for Sample Goals

1. **Goalbook Toolkit.** This interactive website helps you find and create goals in all skill areas at every level of learning. It translates the Common Core standards into concrete and measurable learning goals and references the Common Core standard it's aligned to.
2. **Bridges 4 Kids IEP Goal Bank.** This searchable bank of IEP goals is divided into twelve content areas, each of which are then broken down into the more detailed skills and knowledge that make up each area of content.
3. **IEP Goals, Objectives & Activities App.** This app for iOS was developed by the National Association of Special Education Teachers and contains over 5,000 goals and objectives, as well as activities to use to support each goal.
4. ***800+ Measurable IEP Goals and Objectives for use in K–12 and in Home School Settings*** by Chris de Feyter. This book, also available in electronic form, contains a comprehensive listing of SMART goals that have

been used in classrooms and easily align to your child's present level of performance.

5. *From Gobbledygook to Clearly Written Annual IEP Goals* by Barbara D. Bateman. This book is a good resource, not only for suggestions of goals, but also for helping you walk through the formula of what makes a good goal.

Creating a Goal Chart

Once your child has an IEP in place, it's fairly likely that it will include a Goal chart to keep track of the progress he's making toward his goals. You can make up a different kind of Goal chart to help you in the areas in which you'd like to create sample goals to bring to the table. There's a sample Goal chart in Appendix C, but it's simple enough to make your own as well.

Start by looking at the academic subjects that are covered by your child's classes. For elementary school students, these are typically math, literacy (reading, writing, grammar and spelling combined), science, and social studies. For middle school and high schools students, the academic subjects will vary based on the classes your child is taking, so you'll need a copy of the class schedule to help you out. Next, look at other areas in which your child might need support, including speech and language, motor skills, self-help skills, social-emotional skills, and behavior.

Once you have all of these defined, use your records binder and all the supporting evidence you have gathered to get an idea of what your child's present level of performance (that's the PLOP) is in each area and think about the improvement you'd like to see him make (that is reasonable and realistic) in the next year. Then you can make a Goal chart using that information, like the example shown here, which assumes that John has a number of areas in which he could use some support. That's not always going to be the case; your child may have specific trouble spots and other areas in which he excels.

▼ SAMPLE PARENT GOAL CHART

Subject Area	PLOP	Skills to Work On	Suggested Goal
Reading	John is reading at mid-5th-grade level.	Fluency, vocabulary, reading comprehension.	John will work toward improving his literacy skills to bring his reading level to the beginning of 6th grade.
Math	John is solving multistep word problems at a 4th-grade level.	Understanding operational "cue words," setting up equations.	When given multistep word problems involving the four operations, John will problem-solve to find the solution to the problem.
Speech-Language	John is unable to participate in a turn-taking conversation.	Rules of conversation	John will choose a topic of interest and follow agreed-upon rules for conversation during a three-minute exchange.
Behavior	John is reacting inappropriately to staff and peers when it comes to anger and anxiety.	Coping skills	John will practice and demonstrate appropriate coping strategies to decrease personal anxiety associated with school and peer interactions.

Your Goal chart may not be as detailed or have as specific ideas as to what your child needs to do, but the important part is knowing where your child is having trouble and what skills he needs to learn. Once you've practiced a few times, not only will creating goals become easier, but understanding the goals the school suggests will be easier, too. Remember, though, it's not your responsibility to come up with the goals; it's the job of the entire IEP team. Having them in hand is just one way to prepare for your child's IEP meeting.

CHAPTER 17

Preparing for the
IEP Meeting (Part I)

There are rules about how about IEPs have to be written and there are rules about the rights given to parents and children, so it should not be surprising to know there are rules about the IEP meeting as well. Some of those rules are specifically spelled out by IDEA, and some of them may have been put into place by your school district. It's good to know which rules are in IDEA, because these are rules that have to be followed to make the IEP process legally acceptable.

Rules about Scheduling and Attendance

It's not just good manners to schedule an IEP meeting for a time when you, the parents, can be there. It's also the law. IDEA says that your school district has to give you enough advance notice of a meeting to make sure you're able to be there (or to reschedule) and set the meeting for a mutually agreed upon and convenient time and place. How that actually works in practice varies from school to school.

ALERT

Your school district also needs to have an interpreter on hand if you have a hearing impairment or if English is not your primary language. Let them know ahead of time so they can locate one for the meeting.

Some schools may tell you the times and days on which they hold IEP meetings and expect you to make arrangements so that you can be there on one of those days, while others will give you a choice of various dates and times. Still other schools may simply set a time and date, send you prior written notice, and expect you'll either be there or you won't. If that time is not convenient for you, make sure to speak up. Let the school know you want to be a part of the IEP process and that you know it's your right under IDEA to be there and their responsibility to make every effort for you to be able to attend.

If the school still refuses to change the date and time of the meeting to a mutually convenient time, it's a good idea to write a letter to the school's administrator explaining that you wish to attend your child's IEP meeting, have requested for a change in the meeting time, and that your request has been denied. This letter serves two purposes: It lets the school know you are aware of your rights, and it is on the record that you do not wish to have an IEP written without your being present.

IDEA doesn't have rules about how long a meeting has to be, but it does say it should be scheduled for long enough to cover all the issues. This rarely happens, as meetings are typically scheduled before school, during a teacher's free class period, or for a limited window of time after school. Ideally, you should have at least an hour, if not longer, to make sure that everything that needs to be discussed gets covered. When you get notice of the meeting, if the paperwork doesn't indicate how much time has been set aside, you may want to ask. Once you know how much time you will actually have with all the team members present, you can make a decision as to whether or not you think you need to ask for more time and reschedule the meeting.

Who Should and Can Be There

You already have a good sense of the teachers, providers, and administrators who need to be at an IEP meeting, but IDEA mentions a few other people who may also be there. The first is your child. This whole process is about finding ways to make your child a successful and active participant in her education, but parents and teachers can only do so much to make that happen.

Should Your Child Attend the IEP Meeting?

IDEA says your child should be invited "whenever appropriate." When your child is in elementary school, it's unusual for your child to be able to bring anything new to the table and advocate for her own needs. However, as your child gets older and perhaps a little more independent, the thought is that what she may have to contribute can be important in planning her educational future.

FACT

It's important to recognize that the severity of and limitations presented by some disabilities mean that your child may not always be able to participate in an IEP meeting or make decisions about her own education. That's okay. That's why she has you and your support system on her side.

In fact, as your high-school-age child's transition out of special education is approaching, she is required to be a part of the IEP team to help with planning her future. You may remember that school-based special education services are provided for children between the ages of three and twenty-one. That leaves some flexibility as to when your child will be transitioning out of high school. The majority of children will either graduate or get a certificate of completion by the time they are eighteen years old. For a variety of reasons, some children will be older, and IDEA recognizes that special education services are still necessary to help those older students make a successful transition to the community.

Who Are Individuals "with Special Knowledge?"

The second type of person IDEA says can also be at the IEP meeting is an individual "with knowledge or special expertise" about your child. This person can be invited to an IEP meeting by you or by the school, and IDEA says whoever invites such individuals gets to decide whether they have this knowledge or expertise. It's really not as mysterious as it sounds. If you want a friend, relative, case manager, or advocate to come to the meeting with you, you may invite him. The person (or persons) you bring to the table should know something about your child, your child's educational needs, or how the special education process works as it relates to your child's situation.

The same goes for anybody the school invites who is not legally necessary to be part of the IEP team. For example, if your child has vision impairment or is blind, the school might invite an orientation and mobility specialist to join the meeting as a consultant. This individual doesn't have specific knowledge of your child but does have expertise in an area of need.

Occasionally, the school may invite someone to an IEP meeting who you don't think should be there or who doesn't bring any special knowledge or expertise to the table. The reason why this happens varies; it could be that the school is anticipating a difficult meeting and wants to have a top-level administrator or legal advisor on hand. It could also be that the school has already made a decision about what they would like your child's placement to be and have invited the teacher of that program to be present. Whatever the reasoning, it can be intimidating to be in a room with people who don't know your child, someone with whom you may have clashed in the past, or someone who is there to support an issue that is not on the agenda.

If you are very concerned about a specific participant attending your child's IEP meeting, consider sending a letter of objection. There's a sample letter in Appendix B, but the letter might read something like this:

Dear Mr. Principal,

I have received my prior written notice in regard to Sally's IEP meeting on October 1, 2014. I notice that Dr. S. has been invited to attend this meeting. As far as I am aware, Dr. S. has no knowledge of Sally or unique information that could be helpful to the IEP team.

As you probably know, IEP meetings can be stressful and overwhelming for parents, and adding unnecessary numbers to the table makes it a little more stressful. Therefore, I am formally requesting that she does not attend my child's IEP meeting unless you can provide a specific reason as to why Dr. S.'s presence is necessary to develop or review Sally's IEP.

Should you not provide a reason that her presence is needed and insist that Dr. S. attend this meaning, I will take the more formal step of filing a written complaint with the school district and the Department of Education.

I look forward to hearing from you in regard to this matter.

Respectfully,
Ima Y.

It may seem a little extreme to say that you will file a formal complaint. Realistically, though, if you have a strong enough objection to the individual's presence that you are willing to write a letter about it, filing a complaint is simply a way to formalize your objection.

Alternatives to Traditional Meetings

It used to be that the only way to have an IEP meeting was to do it face-to-face. Working around the schedules of parents, teachers, evaluators, and providers can sometimes make it very difficult to find a time for everyone to attend a meeting. As you attend more IEP meetings, you may notice that there is typically at least one person who is unable to make the meeting because of a scheduling conflict. He may send his thoughts, recommendations, or notes to be read, considered, and entered into the meeting minutes, but it's still not the same as having that person there and available to answer questions.

IDEA 2004 allows for alternative means of holding a meeting. This frequently means a teleconference in which a member of the team calls in to the meeting to participate, but it could also mean video conferencing. This flexibility can make it easier for you to attend a meeting from work or home (if, for example, you're unable to arrange for childcare for another child or are ill) and is a way to avoid delays that can occur when trying to coordinate schedules.

Pros and Cons of Attending via Conference Call

Teleconferences and video conferences have advantages and disadvantages that you'll want to weigh before deciding whether it's the best option for you. The first thing you need to know is whether it's a telephone meeting or teleconference meeting that is being considered.

A telephone meeting is when the phone is used as a way for one or more team members to participate in a meeting. Typically, it's done by putting a phone in the middle of the table and using the phone's speakerphone. Depending on how sophisticated a phone system your child's school has, it's possible to even conference in more than one participant. A teleconference, on the other hand, uses some type of telecommunication device to allow people who are not in the room to participate. This could be via video chat, instant message, e-mail, or by some combination of devices.

ESSENTIAL

There are three advantages to teleconference meetings: 1) They give parents a chance to participate without feeling intimidated by being seated with a group of professionals; 2) they allow parents to participate, even if travel and schedules present issues; and 3) they avoid delays due to a team member's unavailability.

Another thing to consider is who will be attending by phone. If it's you, and you're more likely to feel comfortable speaking your mind when you're not surrounded by school personnel, it might be worth giving it a try. For the most part, though, the disadvantages of attending a meeting by teleconference may outweigh the benefits. Many of the same things that can be intimidating to you during a face-to-face meeting can also be helpful and may get lost in translation during a phone call. Consider these factors:

Body Language and Nonverbal Communication

When you're sitting in a meeting, you can often tell what the other members of the IEP team are thinking by watching their faces or posture while someone is talking. That can certainly be intimidating if the message you're getting is that what you're saying isn't important or that people disagree with you, but it also serves the purpose of giving you the chance to say things like, "I notice that you made a face when I suggested we try this approach. Can you explain what your concern is?" Over the phone or via video conference, you will not be able to see these subtle indicators of the mood of the room.

Interactions Between Team Members

Just as you have considered what you want to get accomplished at the IEP meeting, the school has, too. That may mean that teachers and administrators have had sort of a "premeeting meeting" in which they discussed certain portions of an evaluation or talked about what each team member will bring up at the meeting. Sometimes in face-to-face meetings you will see interactions between team members, like somebody writing a note on a pad of paper, pointing to a certain paragraph in a report, or even giving a little nod or headshake to each other. You may not understand what those interactions mean, but they're important to pay attention to. These interactions cannot be observed during a teleconference or telephone meeting.

Knowing Who's Who

When you're sitting at a meeting, you're able to place a face to each person as he or she speaks. Additionally, in a phone conference, even if people introduce themselves, they often forget to continue to identify themselves as the meeting gets going. You may end up spending so much energy trying to figure out who is speaking that you're unable to pay attention to what is being said.

Jargon and Document Review

Another thing that can get lost in translation is your ability to ask other team members to explain the terms they are using, show you the document that's being referred to, or even ask an evaluator to talk more in depth about a specific piece of an evaluation report. It also means that school personnel aren't able to tell when you might be getting lost in the jargon. When everybody is sitting around the table, it's easier for people to speak up and say, "I'm sorry, what that means is . . . " or "Can you explain what that means?" Despite these factors, if a teleconference is the only way that you are able to attend your child's IEP meeting, it's better than not being a part of the process at all.

When It's Okay to Forgo an Annual Meeting

After your child's initial IEP is written, it will be reviewed annually. The annual meeting is to talk about your child's progress toward his goals, review how things are going, and make any changes to the IEP that seem reasonable based on all of that information. In some cases, you will find that nothing has changed much from last year. Your child's goals are still appropriate, the services he has in place are exactly what he needs, and there's nothing really new to talk about. If that's the case, you probably already know that before the annual meeting, both because you've been getting regular progress reports and because if there was a significant problem, either the school got in touch with you or you got in touch with the school.

When everything is going as planned, IDEA allows for you to forgo the annual meeting and make changes to the IEP in writing, as long as both you and the school agree to it. Just make sure you have a copy of your child's current IEP to compare to the new one before you sign it. If there are any changes, you'll want to make sure you understand what they mean before signing a new IEP. Don't hesitate to ask questions!

Questions to Ask about the Meeting

Not all parents are comfortable asking questions. It can be overwhelming because if you don't know or understand something, it can be hard to even figure out what it is you're trying to figure out. The paperwork and language involved in special education can make that even tougher sometimes. Here are some questions to ask that are specific to the IEP meeting:

1. **Why are we meeting?** The answer to this should be on the prior written notice, but you may not understand all the options or what they mean. After all, someone who works in special education may understand how the box marked "Initial Referral" is different than the box marked "Consent for Initial Placement," but many parents will not.

2. **Who is actually going to be there?** The prior written notice you received lists the people who were invited to your child's IEP meeting, but that doesn't mean they will all be able to attend. It's a good idea to follow up with the IEP coordinator to find out who will be there, especially if you really feel a certain participant has important information to add. That way if you find out that person had a scheduling conflict, you can request the meeting be rescheduled to a day and time when he is able to attend.

3. **Do I have the most recent progress reports or provider notes?** This question may not be relevant if you are meeting to develop an IEP, but it's certainly relevant if you're going to an annual meeting or a meeting in which changes to your child's program are being proposed. If there is no new documented information about your child since the last time you met, there really shouldn't be any reason to change anything in the IEP. That means if the school wants to make changes, they need to have something to back it up. The prior written notice should list what the school is using as basis for wanting changes. Check that list against your records binder—if you don't have everything, then before the meeting takes place is the time to ask for it.

4. **Is there anything else I should be aware of?** This is a very broad question on purpose. Sometimes a teacher will bring something up at an IEP meeting—an incident that happened in class or a new skill your child has acquired, for example—that you knew nothing about. If that information is going to play a role in any decision the IEP team makes, it's probably something you should know before you sit down at the table. Asking if there's anything you should be aware of or the even more general, "How is my child doing?" may ward off the surprise and frustration that can come with finding out something big that everybody else already knew.

Giving the School the Benefit of the Doubt

When you're sitting down to look at evaluations, programs, goals, and services, it can feel as though you're the only one on your child's side. This is often exacerbated by the stories other people tell you about their dealings with a school and how hard they had to fight to get special education services for their child. While many people tell these stories, it's important to keep in mind that stories about when things went well are much less dramatic and not as often told.

When an IEP team works together to create a program that's best for a child, writes appropriate goals, and then the child thrives in the environment, it's not a story parents tend to tell. But it doesn't mean that doesn't happen. Unless you've been given reason otherwise, giving the school the benefit of the doubt can make a big difference, not only in easing your feelings about a potentially confrontational situation, but also to make an IEP more comfortable for all the participants. Ultimately, an IEP meeting is about making sure your child is successfully educated, and most teachers really want that to happen. Focusing on your child's needs and expecting that all the other team members around the table are there to do the same can set a positive tone for the meeting.

Going into a meeting with the attitude that your child's teachers have her best interests at heart can make it easier to present your position objectively without placing blame and without anyone feeling attacked. You can be a strong advocate for your child without being defensive, especially if you've done your research, you speak up when you don't understand something, and you keep in mind that you have as much to contribute as the other people around the table.

CHAPTER 18

Preparing for the IEP Meeting (Part II)

IEP meetings can be emotionally draining for parents. After all, even though the conversation is centered on evaluations, services, programs, and progress, what you're all really talking about is your child. Trying to make sure that everybody remembers there's a real child behind all the numbers and evidence can be stressful. When you factor in the time constraints of most IEP meetings, it can be difficult to be certain you have the time to fully discuss what needs to be discussed educationally and paint an accurate picture of your child's personality and temperament. In order to make sure you get that accomplished, preparing for the IEP meeting will involve more than just knowing your rights and the rules of the meeting.

Know Your Stuff, Know Your Position

You may have identified what the school's position or preferences for your child's program are, and you may have drafted your ideal IEP. Before you go into a meeting, it's a good idea to make sure you know what your own position is, too. That involves more than just knowing what services you'd like your child to have, having some goals in mind, or even knowing a specific class you'd like your child to be placed in. Knowing your position is about being able to clearly state your beliefs, wishes, and thoughts about your child's education. It's based not only on what all the paperwork says about her, but also based on your special knowledge of your child. If you remember, "special knowledge" is IDEA's phrase about the people who are invited to an IEP meeting.

ESSENTIAL

All the preparations for an IEP meeting can be overwhelming, but once you've done it a few times it gets easier. You'll have a better idea of the process and what to expect. You also will have a good start on a records binder and won't have to start from scratch every time.

As a parent, you have special knowledge and insight into your child that nobody else can provide. You are the one who knows what happens when she sits down to do homework at the end of the day. You are the one who knows how it's going on the bus to and from school every day. You are the one who knows the cumulative impact of her struggles in school or with friends over the years and how that affects her attitude toward school and herself. You are the person who is likely to know whether your child will work well with a specific teacher or service provider based on personality and prior experience. All of that knowledge that comes from being an integral part of your child's life for her entire life is important and is factored into your position.

There are other considerations that help make up your position as well, some of which have to do with your child's age and specific disability, some of which have to do with the related services you know are available, and some of which have to do with your beliefs about education in general. Some things to consider include:

- **What are your feelings about mainstreaming or inclusion in the regular education classroom?** What you should consider here is how strongly you feel about your child being included (or not included) in the regular education classroom. For some children this won't even be an issue because accommodations and modifications can be made in the classroom. For others, though, it's a very real issue. If your child is significantly behind her peers academically or functionally or has a disability (such as autism) that makes it hard for her to learn in a typical way, you'll need to weigh the pros and cons of inclusion. Keep in mind that it doesn't have to be all or nothing; there are ways to include your child even if it's not for the academic portion of the day.

- **What do you know about the related services the school provides?** Your ideal IEP outlines what an ideal situation would look like for your child, but you need to be prepared for compromise. That means knowing what's really available. For instance, you might want your child to have time with an occupational therapist a few times a week, but if the school district only employs a certified occupational therapy assistant (COTA), you cannot expect them to hire an occupational therapist to work with your child. The therapist's credentials may not be exactly what you want, but they are acceptable in terms of providing the services your child needs.

- **Where will you hold the line?** This is an incredibly important and incredibly difficult question to consider. You will probably have to make compromises and give up parts of your ideal IEP based on what the school (and IDEA) thinks is appropriate for your child. That doesn't mean you have to give up or give in completely. You've created an ideal IEP, but it's prudent to also have an idea of what a "good enough" IEP would look like to you. Know what you will stand firm on and what is not important. This is easier to do if you keep in mind that it's not about winning—it's about making sure your child is getting a free appropriate public education.

There are also some special circumstances in which you need to know the typical procedures and rules before going in to talk about what you want for your child.

Transitioning from Early Intervention to School-Based Services

Your child's transition from early intervention to school-based services (or from Part C to Part B) will happen before kindergarten. When she turns three, she moves from an individual family service plan (IFSP) with a service coordinator to an individualized education program (IEP) in a preschool setting. This transition can be a big adjustment for a number of reasons.

Firstly, the services are provided differently. Instead of home-based services, your child's services are based in an educational setting. In some states your child will have to be in a preschool or Head Start program, but in other states that's not the case. What is the same across the board is your child's program is now based on her educational needs; the services are not family focused, they are school focused.

That's important to keep in mind as you attend the IFSP to IEP transition meeting when you are thinking about your position in regard to your child's education. You need to make the shift between thinking about what your child and family need for support in her everyday living to what support your child needs to have the same education as nondisabled peers. It's a hard shift to make, especially since it may feel as though your child is too young to start thinking about her needs from a school perspective.

Secondly, when your child moves from Part C to Part B, she must meet the eligibility requirements of IDEA. Those eligibility requirements are the thirteen categories of disability that school-age children can be found eligible under, with the added category of "developmental delay" for three-year-olds and four-year-olds. Developmental delay is only used if: (a) your child's delays in development, as measured by evaluation, are significant enough to affect her ability to participate in preschool or "age-relevant activities" and (b) those delays cannot be attributed to a specific disability.

The good news is that IDEA says your service coordinator has to start the transition process at least six months before your child's third birthday. That means there is time for re-evaluations of your child's skills, time to look at preschool programs, and time to talk about whether your child will be eligible for services under Part B. Even better news is that even if your child is not eligible for Part B services, there must be a transition plan in place anyway that includes other options for your child. Those other options might include things like services that are paid for by your child's insurance plan or community programs.

Transferring to a Private School

If your child is transferring to a private school, what happens with your child's IEP is dependent on the circumstances surrounding the transfer. If he is transferring because the public school agreed it's the best placement for your child, the placing school district is responsible for making sure services are transferred and in place. If you are voluntarily placing your child in a private school, he may still be able to receive limited special education services from the local public school district. The services are limited and based on a consultation with the local private school about the special education needs of the children enrolled and subject to a complicated proportionate funding formula. At its simplest, if you choose to enroll your child in private school, your child is not legally entitled to receive the same level of special education services from the local school district that he would receive if he were enrolled in public school.

Transferring from Another School District

Another special circumstance that can affect your position is transferring from a different school district in which your child already had an IEP. Luckily, when IDEA was written this possibility was taken into consideration, and there are rules about what has to happen. If you move into a different school district in the same state, the new school district is obligated to provide a program with services "comparable" to what is on your child's current IEP until a new IEP is created. If you move to another state, the new school district has the same obligation, but it has the option to do a comprehensive educational evaluation of your child before creating a new IEP.

The word "comparable" is worth paying attention to. It does not mean "exactly the same," it means that your child's program needs to be as similar as possible to what it was before you moved. There has to be a little room to account for the fact that school districts have different types of programs and classrooms. That doesn't mean you have to agree to a program that will not be as effective for your child or that doesn't have the same services. It means you may need to look at things a little more flexibly.

For example, if your child previously had three hours of direct speech-language services broken into four, forty-five minute sessions a week, it wouldn't be unreasonable for the new school to provide three, one-hour sessions a week. It adds up to the same amount of time. On the other hand, if the new school district decided to provide speech-language services to your child in a group, that's not comparable because your child's IEP specified direct (or one-on-one) services.

ALERT

IDEA says a new school must attempt to get your child's school records and IEP from the old school "promptly," but promptly isn't defined. In order to make sure your child's IEP is followed, it's a good idea to hand-deliver a copy of your child's records when you register at the new school.

High School Transition Planning

Another circumstance to keep in mind is the transition planning that needs to take place no later than your child's sixteenth birthday. Even if your meeting is to develop the very first IEP your child has ever had, if your child is sixteen or older, the IEP must provide postsecondary goals. That means well-thought-out goals about what your child will be doing after high school, and what services and classes she will need to be able to meet those goals. There are three areas that need to be looked at when it comes to transition planning: education/training, employment, and independent living. Those are the same areas that IDEA says your child's education should be preparing her for.

Transition goals should be measurable and realistic, which means you have to take into account your child's abilities and what she will realistically be able to learn after she is done with high school. Some examples of measurable and realistic transition goals are:

- After completing high school, John will attend classes at the local community college.

- John will get a part-time job with the assistance of a postsecondary career counselor who specializes in working with young adults with disabilities.
- John will learn to use the bus system in order to attend classes at the local community college.

Organize, Organize, and Organize!

Once you feel comfortable that you are able to state your position clearly, it's time to make sure you have everything for the meeting—both to back up your position and to keep track of what's going on. Assuming you've gone through your child's records and evaluations, have gone through the IEP Preparation Checklist, and have made a records binder (see Appendix C for the sample forms), you have a good start on having what you need to support your case. Organize it in a way that makes sense to you and have copies of the important documents in case the school wants to see them. It may not seem like it makes sense to make copies of documents that came from your child's education records, but it's possible that the school will not have all of your child's information easily available at the IEP meeting. It's better to be able to hand a school representative a copy than to have to reschedule a meeting because someone needs to find it and look it over.

ESSENTIAL

You may want to consider bringing a note taker with you to the meeting. It's hard to participate and keep up while you're taking careful notes.

Getting organized also means being prepared to take careful notes of the meeting, especially if you anticipate disagreement amongst team members. Have a notepad or notebook and something to write with handy. Some parents prefer to bring a laptop or audiotape meetings, but it's not always easy to pay attention to the nonverbal interactions at a meeting while you're typing on a laptop. Likewise, an audiotape will provide a record of what everybody said, but it doesn't give you the chance to make notes about who said it, how they looked when they said it, and what you were thinking while it was said.

There will be a school-designated note taker who will create meeting minutes, but those minutes will only include highlights of what was discussed at the meeting. What you think is important to highlight may not be the same as what school personnel thinks is important to highlight.

Things to Highlight in Your Notes

It's not practical to think you'll be able to write down everything that happens at the IEP meeting. Keep a copy of your ideal IEP handy or give one to your note taker so you can take notes about things that relate to it. If you can, it's helpful to write down not only what was said but also who said it. Other things to keep track of are comments about your child's progress that aren't written down anywhere, anecdotes that teachers share to illustrate how your child is doing, specific program and service recommendations, and reasons for those recommendations. It's especially important to take notes about things that cause friction; if you ever have to make a complaint or file for mediation or due process, you'll have an independent record of the meeting.

Practice Your Rebuttal Skills

IEP meetings can be intimidating, especially if you're not used to them. Being an advocate for your child means you may sometimes have to stand your ground, stand up for yourself, or stand up for your child's rights. That can be a very uncomfortable position to be in. Under the best of circumstances, you will be in a meeting full of people who genuinely care about providing a good education for your child and are understanding of how overwhelming the process can be for parents. A team like this is willing to help you through the process and have reasonable discussions.

In some circumstances, however, you may run up against people who are abrasive, rude, and deliberately intimidating. Practicing your rebuttal skills is a good way to be prepared to respond to rude and inflammatory remarks. It can help you feel less steamrolled and give you back some control.

Sometimes the best rebuttal to a provocative remark is to just not respond or provide a simple acknowledgment. A nod of the head or a calm "I see," is an easy way to acknowledge that you heard what was said without saying you agree. On other occasions, you may find that what you're hearing is personally insulting, condescending, or just wrong, and you need to address either the tone or the content of what was said. Some examples of comments that you might hear and need to respond to are:

- "No, you're wrong about that."
- "That's not what the law says/ that's not what the law means by that."
- "You don't understand what the report is really saying."
- "I don't expect you to understand how this works."
- "Maybe you could get another school to do that, but we're not going to do it here."
- "I think we're just done talking about that."
- "I'm not sure where you're getting your information."
- "That's not the school's job; that's your job."
- "I'm not agreeing to that."

How you respond will depend on what bothers you about the comment—the tone or the content. In many cases, it's likely to be both. Typically, if you're objecting to what someone is saying, it's probably not being said all that nicely, either.

What you can practice at home before the meeting is keeping as calm and reasonable as possible, which is not always easy when you're feeling attacked. If you can't keep your voice from shaking, that's okay, but yelling or being nasty in return takes away from what you have to say.

For situations in which you're offended by how you're being spoken to, you can use a response such as, "I don't appreciate your tone of voice. I'm treating you respectfully and expect the same in return" or "I'm not sure why you're being so hostile. We may not agree, but there's no reason not to be civil about it."

When you have an objection to the content of a comment as well, you can add on to one of the other rebuttal phrases. For instance: "I don't appreciate your tone of voice. I'm treating you respectfully and expect the same in return. You're right; I don't understand what the report is saying, but I'd really like to. Could you please explain what it means and why it's important?" or "I'm getting my information from the evaluation the school did. I'm not sure why you're being so hostile. We may not agree, but there's no reason not to be civil about it."

When a person persists in being aggressive or hostile, you may need to take a harder line with something along the lines of, "I'm not going to allow you to continue to speak to me in such a rude/disrespectful/condescending way. If this is the way the meeting is going to continue, I think we're going to need to adjourn and ask that [the special education director or superintendent] join us when we sit down again." This makes it clear that not only are you not going to engage, but that you'll also be bringing the behavior to the attention of the appropriate personnel.

Having Your Own Advocate

Some parents hesitate to use the word "advocate" or to bring one with them to a meeting because they're afraid it will set an adversarial tone from the beginning. But it doesn't have to be that way. An advocate is simply someone who is there to support you and help speak up for your child's rights and needs. You can be a very good advocate for your child, but you have a lot of emotional investment in the outcome of a meeting.

No matter how well you know the law or how comfortable you feel holding your own with the professionals, you don't want to underestimate the effect of hearing people debate your child's strengths and weaknesses. It can be very hard to respond to statements about your child without having an emotional reaction—and you shouldn't have to set that aside; it's that feeling for your child that drives you to make sure he has what he needs to be successful and happy. Having someone else at the meeting with you who is willing to make sure your child's rights are protected can give you a little room to respond more emotionally.

Is a Friend an Advocate?

For the first IEP meeting or a meeting in which you're not anticipating disagreement between you and the school, your advocate doesn't necessarily need to be someone well-versed in special education. It can be your partner or spouse, a friend, or a relative you trust. In that case the person you bring is there as support for you, not as someone who can necessarily speak up for your child. That person's role as advocate is to be another set of ears to hear what's going on, to take notes if you wish, and to be there to give you a little more confidence.

ALERT

Any time you are bringing an advocate or support person who is not listed on the IEP invitation, it's a good idea to inform the school in advance. The school has the right to challenge the person's "special knowledge" of your child. Without prior warning, this can delay or postpone a meeting.

When you bring a friend or relative with you, it's a good idea to have a premeeting with that person. Brief him about the issues your child is having in school (if he's not already aware of them), ask him to be your note taker, and talk with him about what kind of support you are looking for. For the most part, unless your support person has a unique perspective about your child that can add beneficial information for the IEP team, he won't be expected to speak. Do, however, talk with him about what you want to bring up at the meeting and have him carry those points with him, so he can remind you of anything you forget. Also, keep in mind that your appearance and that of your support person will make an impression on the IEP team as well. You may want to take the time to talk about appropriate meeting attire.

Finding an Educational Advocate

In some cases, bringing a special education advocate or IEP advocate with you to a meeting is a better choice than simply bringing a support person with you. This is especially true if you've had difficulty navigating the special education process and have not found the school to be an ally or if other parents have told you the school is difficult to work with. Or, you might just feel as though you don't have enough knowledge to make sure your child gets the services she needs to ensure a free appropriate public education. There's nothing wrong in reaching out to someone who is more experienced and knowledgeable about the process.

Advocates undergo specialized training to learn more about the special education process. Some are also part of parent advocacy networks and have become incredibly familiar with the IEP process by going through it themselves. There are a few ways to go about finding a special education advocate in your area. You can begin by getting in touch with the federally funded State Parent Training and Information Center in your state to ask about advocacy groups. You can also get in touch with the National Disability Rights Network or the Council of Parent Attorneys and Advocates, Inc. (COPAA). All of these groups are able to direct you to an advocate or advocacy center in your area. Not all educational advocates donate their time, though, so you should consider asking for a list of names so you can speak with a number of people. Choose someone who you can afford, who you feel comfortable talking to, and who you feel is listening to you.

A good relationship between a parent and an educational advocate is important. Your educational advocate is there to help you make sure an appropriate IEP is written and to ensure that your child gets special education services from the school district. An advocate can be very helpful in negotiations between parents and schools. The advocate you work with will be familiar with the resources of your school district and might be able to find solutions that you cannot. An advocate serves many roles and can help you:

- Understand the special education process
- Read school records, assessments, and other information to find what is important
- Organize your materials and records binder
- Write letters to school officials or the Department of Education as necessary
- Talk to the school about appropriate assessments, your child's current level of performance, and measurable goals
- Present your thoughts and position at an IEP meeting
- Learn to be a more effective advocate for your child

It is important to keep in mind that special education advocates are not attorneys, and in some situations you may need to have an attorney assist you instead of a special education advocate.

Do You Need an Attorney?

An attorney (also known as a lawyer) can help you with many of the same things as a special education advocate. Usually parents don't consider hiring a lawyer until things get adversarial and there's the potential that you or the school district might file for mediation or a due process hearing. If you and the school district are in disagreement about what services are best for your child, that's not automatically a reason to bring in a lawyer. If you and the school district are in disagreement and they bring their lawyer to the table, you definitely should think about bringing your own attorney with you as well.

Since an attorney can be expensive and bringing one to the table can escalate things, there are some things to consider before bringing one on board. The first is to make sure that the lawyer you are considering hiring specializes in education law. A real estate lawyer or a criminal attorney is not going to be of much help when it comes to knowing the nuances of IDEA. Beyond that, you will also want to make sure that an attorney has some knowledge of your child's specific disability and how it can impact learning. Other things to consider if you are asking an attorney to take on your child's case and begin legal action are:

How Complicated Is Your Child's Case?

The question here is what it is that you and the school are in disagreement about and whether you feel as though you really understand the issues at stake. If you're disagreeing about a service provider, that's something an advocate can probably help you with. If you're having trouble agreeing on placement and services at all, the advice of an attorney is probably a better idea.

What Are You Trying to Accomplish?

Sometimes parents and schools can get so caught up in fighting about who is right that they lose sight of the ultimate goal. If you are fighting for something that your child needs and will be beneficial to her education, that's a good reason to bring an attorney on board. If you're fighting to show the school district they "can't get away with this" and the end result won't help your child, it may be better to speak to an attorney about filing a complaint or simply sitting down at the table with you. Remember that taking legal action in regard to your child's IEP can take a long time, and while the process is playing itself out, your child's services cannot be changed. That means if the program she has in place isn't helping her, it will remain that way until the court makes a decision.

Can You Afford Representation?

This is a frustrating element to have to consider, especially when you're trying to do what's best for your child, but it's one to consider nonetheless. If you need an attorney to make sure your child gets the services for a FAPE and don't think you can afford one, speak to parent advocacy groups or disability organizations about nonprofit legal clinics in your area. Appendix D has a list of parent groups, organizations, and resources you can turn to for assistance.

If you decide you need an attorney to help you but aren't sure whether or not you have a case, ask potential lawyers to do a case review. The lawyer will look over the evidence and records and provide you with an honest opinion of how strong your case and evidence is. He will let you know what other evidence you might need, and let you know how much work and expense is likely to be involved in the case.

It's worth noting that once you bring an attorney into the mix, your relationship with the school district is likely to change. School personnel may be less comfortable speaking with you without attorneys present or they may feel defensive. Those are not reasons not to hire a lawyer. If you do not feel as though your child's right to a free appropriate public education is being met, that is a more important point than whether or not the school district likes you.

CHAPTER 19

Attending and Participating in an IEP Meeting

You've looked over the evaluations, gone over progress reports, and spoken with teachers. You've thought about what you'd like your child's program to look like, weighed the pros and cons of various programs, and have an idea of how to respond to awkward comments or situations. You've chosen a support person or attorney and have talked about everybody's role and responsibilities. Grab your records binder, your notepad, your audio recorder (if you're bringing one), and your support person—it's time for the IEP meeting.

Arriving at the Meeting

Being on time to an IEP meeting is very important. It shows that you are invested in the process and take everybody's time seriously. You may even want to get there ten to fifteen minutes before the meeting starts. That will give you time to find a seat—meetings can be crowded—get comfortable with the meeting space, organize your materials, gauge the mood of the room, get the audio recorder set up, and exchange greetings with the other IEP team members. It also means you won't have to walk into a room full of people already sitting down and waiting for you to get there and get organized. IEP meetings can be very involved, and starting them on time is key in making sure they're not rushed and everything that needs to be discussed comes up.

ESSENTIAL

Bring a bottle of water with you to your meeting. You'll be talking a lot, and being nervous can make your mouth dry.

If you don't know everybody in the room, it's perfectly acceptable to introduce yourself and ask other people their names and how they know your child. It's also okay to acknowledge that you're nervous; it humanizes you and serves as a reminder that you and your child are real people whose lives will be affected by the outcome of this meeting. Saying something as simple as "I'm sorry my hands are so sweaty/cold, I'm a little anxious about being here today," may help to defuse some of the tension or soften any preconceived notions a teacher may have about you.

You may not have an opportunity to introduce yourself to all the people in the room before the meeting begins, but the first order of business on the agenda should be introductions. That's exactly what it sounds like—each person around the table will have the chance to say his or her name and role in your child's education.

Parents Are Team Members, Too

There's no better time than introductions to establish that you are aware you are a member of the IEP team. How you choose to introduce yourself can set the tone for your participation in the meeting. Consider the difference between saying, "I'm Ima. I'm just John's mom," and "I'm Ima. I'm John's mom." That word "just" implies that you don't think you're as important or have as much to offer as anyone else on the team. It sets the stage for other people to treat you like "just John's mom" instead of as an equal participant with valuable information and insights to add.

The same goes for your child if he's attending the meeting—he should be introduced and expect that people will talk to him, not just about him. Some teachers and parents ask that kids begin attending at least a portion of the IEP meeting once they are of middle school age. That's because when your child gets to middle school, the expectation is that he will be a more independent and active participant in his education.

This depends, to some degree, on how your child's disability affects him intellectually and functionally. If he's able to understand why he has an IEP and what it means, it's not a bad idea to include him for some of the meeting. After all, he will be the one working with teachers and service providers toward meeting his goals. He should have an opportunity to at least hear what the expectations are. Until he's of the age of majority, though, the IEP team does not need him to give his approval to the plan.

Eight IEP Dos and Don'ts

Every meeting is different, but there are some basics of etiquette that you should try to stick to. It's easier to remember them as the dos and don'ts of a meeting. Hopefully, everyone in the meeting follows these basic rules.

1. DO be respectful of other people's opinions. Being rude or attacking a person for her opinion will not be helpful in coming to an agreement. It's more likely to make other people defensive and not as willing to listen to your own opinions.
2. DON'T accept opinion as a fact. Feel free to ask for clarification or for the evidence that backs up an opinion.
3. DO ask questions. If there's something you don't understand, speak up. You're probably not the only person around the table who doesn't understand, and even if you are, you have to completely understand what's going on to make informed decisions about your child's education.

4. DON'T be intimidated. Staying silent because you're worried about what people will think or because you think the professionals know best is more likely to lead to resentment and misunderstandings.

5. DO give people the benefit of the doubt. Making accusations or assuming that the school is going to oppose your ideas just because they can isn't fair. Unless you have clear reason to believe otherwise, it's better to assume that everybody there wants to help your child.

6. DON'T be accusatory. Even if you encounter differing opinions or opposition, try to stay firm but fair. Until you ask directly about the motives behind a decision or opinion, you can't know for sure what somebody else is thinking.

7. DO keep your temper. It's okay to be emotional at an IEP meeting, and it's even okay to cry; most people will be sympathetic and understand that it is difficult to sit in a meeting and hear about your child's weaknesses. But it's essential to keep your temper under control. It may not be easy to do, especially if you feel like your parenting is being questioned, you're not being listened to, or an inaccurate picture is being painted of your child. But losing your temper may also cause your point to be lost as well.

8. DON'T hesitate to disagree. If you think a goal isn't appropriate, you have every right to say so. If you think a teacher isn't seeing the full scope of your child's limitations, speak up and explain what other teachers have seen in the past and what you see at home. Disagreement doesn't necessarily have to cause strife. It's a way to make sure all the issues and angles are thoroughly explored.

Choosing Battles and Words Wisely

Knowing what issues to explore and how to talk about them makes a big difference at a meeting, too. There are some phrases or words that you can use that may actually hurt your case when you're talking about services and programs, such as "best," "ideal," or "optimal." For example, if you disagree with a program suggestion, it's not a good idea to say you're rejecting it because it's "not the ideal program" or "best educational setting" for your child. It's better to say you don't think it's an "appropriate program" or that it's an "inappropriate educational setting."

The difference in phrasing may seem small, but it will signal to the school that you are aware of what IDEA requires of them. If you recall, IDEA doesn't say your child has to have the optimal or ideal program to meet her educational needs. IDEA only says your child has to have an "appropriate" education. Talking about programs in terms of being best or optimal gives the school district the opening to say you are expecting more for your child than the law requires them to provide. Speaking in terms of appropriateness lets the school district know that you don't think what they are suggesting meets their legal obligation to your child.

Your battles should also be chosen as carefully as your words. Sometimes that means stepping back and admitting that the case you are making for a particular program or service isn't as strong as you thought it was. Or it may mean that the school district presented a solution you didn't think of that will meet your child's needs just as well as what you were advocating for. It could be that you need to let go of arguing about how a particular goal or accommodation is worded in order to have time to make bigger decisions, like the classroom or program in which your child will be placed. Asking yourself, "Why is this important?" can help you decide whether you're staying focused on making this meeting about your child's education.

Asking Questions and Challenging Assertions

It may seem as though you're going to be the one who is always making compromises, but that's not the case. Just because you're choosing battles wisely doesn't mean there aren't battles worth fighting. And how you word questions can help you fight those battles. A well-worded question can be a good way to convince others that your position is worth considering.

For instance, if you think it would be better for your child to remain in the regular education classroom with a one-to-one aide and the evaluator's report supports that, you can state your position as a question. "We've all read the evaluator's report, correct? In it he states that John would benefit from extra assistance to help him with math. He also states that it's his belief that John would benefit from continued interaction with his nondisabled, grade-level peers and that it's likely John wouldn't tolerate a transition to a new classroom this late in the school year. Given this, don't you agree that a one-to-one aide in the regular education classroom would be the best and least restrictive option?"

You will probably not be the only one who uses statements and questions as a way to persuade people to consider a position. Sometimes, administrators or teachers will use what's known as a "blanket assertion" to head you off. A *blanket assertion* is a statement that is presented as fact without any attempt to prove why it's accurate. Some common assertions at IEP meetings include:

- That service/program costs too much.
- We have to consider how your child's disability/behavior is affecting the education of the other children in the classroom.
- Providing that service for your child means another child will have to go without services.
- That's not a service we provide.
- We're not allowed to discuss that.
- It's our policy to do it that way.
- That's just the way things are.
- That's not the law.
- As a general rule . . .

As you can see, each of these statements sounds authoritative, but without anything to back them up they're not necessarily logical. In some cases, they may not even be legal. This is particularly true with the assertions that try to cut off conversation about services that your child needs but are expensive for the school district. While it may be true that the service "costs too much" and will put a strain on the school budget, IDEA requires a discussion of the services that are needed to provide your child with an appropriate education. Monetary concerns are not a valid reason to refuse to discuss or provide a service. It is also not appropriate to bring up other children's services or educational needs as a way to stop conversation or convince you to agree to a placement you don't think is appropriate for your child.

It is completely appropriate for you to challenge such assertions, and you can do so in a very direct, nonconfrontational way. For instance: "I am aware that there are other children in need of services and other children in the classroom, but we're here to discuss my child's needs. The law is clear that the conversation we should be having is about appropriate services and the least restrictive environment for my child, not the how much that would cost or the effect on other children."

Challenging other assertions can be even simpler than that. When you're facing a statement about policy, rules, or law, ask to see a copy of the policy or the law and why that's the policy. If the stated policy isn't in writing or doesn't seem to comply with what IDEA requires of schools, you don't have to (and shouldn't) let the issue drop. You don't have to continue arguing with the administrator, but you can make it clear you will be asking the same questions of school officials in a higher-level position.

Moving a Meeting Along

For the most part, IEP meetings tend to move at a brisk pace because there's so much information to cover in a limited amount of time. The law doesn't limit the amount of time available for a meeting; it's typically people's schedules that impose time limits. There are certainly disadvantages to having a short period of time allotted for a meeting—mainly that there's not enough time to get into great detail about your child and his needs. Everybody on the IEP team has a chance to speak to express observations, concerns, and opinions, which can take up a fair amount of time, and that's just the beginning of the meeting.

A Typical IEP Meeting Agenda

All meetings are different, but they typically follow similar agendas. For the most part, that looks like:

1. Introductions are made and the purpose of the meeting is stated.
2. Parents are given a copy of *Parental Rights and Procedural Safeguards* and are asked if there are any questions.
3. Recent evaluations and assessments are reviewed and explained or reports on progress are given by your child's teachers.
4. The floor is opened for questions or comments about the assessment and progress reports.
5. Parents are asked to provide information, talk about their child, and bring up any concerns.
6. At an initial meeting, eligibility and the category of disability are discussed; at an annual meeting, the category of disability is reviewed.

7. Present level of performance in all areas, including academics, functioning, and behavior, are discussed and determined. If your child is sixteen or older, your child's goals for after high school will also be discussed.

8. SMART goals are created with input from the entire team, or current goals are reviewed and revised as necessary.

9. A discussion about services and placement to best carry out those goals will ensue.

10. Other items such as accommodations, modifications, assistive technology, and behavior plans will be discussed and decided upon.

11. There will be a conversation about what will happen next and another meeting will be discussed or scheduled if possible or necessary.

12. An overview/summary of the meeting will be provided and the meeting will be adjourned.

As you can see, that's a lot of information to cover. It leaves room for a lot of debate and conversation, and it can be easy for a big chunk of the meeting time to be taken up by talking about generalities and theory. That gives you two very important reasons to keep track of the time.

ALERT

If you anticipate the meeting will take a long time and your child's teacher will have to leave, ask in advance for the school to have a substitute available to watch the classroom for the duration of the IEP meeting.

The first is that when time is limited, it can be tempting for administrators to give each person only a short amount of time to talk. The second is that you want to make sure everybody is present to talk about the specifics of your child's program. If a meeting is scheduled before school, it's also not unusual for classroom teachers to have to leave partway through the meeting. This means that the whole team is not there to make crucial decisions about your child's program, which can be detrimental if you were counting on a particular team member being there to support your views.

Ways to Keep It Moving

If it looks as though time is running short, you will have to make a decision as to whether you want to try to move the meeting along or whether you want to ask to continue the meeting at another time. When it looks as though everything can be accomplished in the time you have left, you can simply mention that you are concerned you will run out of time and that you would like to move on to talking about the specifics of goals and services. Sometimes you will find that a meeting is dragging because a team member has a specific incident or question to discuss with you. If what that team member wants to discuss doesn't really have bearing on the IEP, it's okay to suggest that you set up a separate time to talk about it.

What Not to Do to Try to Save Time

Don't make sacrifices to make sure an IEP is written in the meeting time you have. That means making sure that everybody—including you—has enough time to explain his or her thoughts fully and ask all the questions he or she needs to ask. If you're feeling rushed or cut off, speak up and let people know you have more questions or more you'd like to say.

ALERT

Saving time isn't always the best thing to do. Some children have very involved needs, and the team needs a lot of time to talk about all of them to come up with a well-thought-out educational plan. Ask for more time or for a second meeting if it's needed.

Not making sacrifices also means you shouldn't agree to things you aren't comfortable with just to make sure the rest of the IEP is written. It's okay to ask to take some time to think about a service that's being offered or a particularly tricky issue. It doesn't mean the whole meeting has to stop, either. It just means that you will need to reconvene to talk about that one piece of the IEP. Or, if after taking a few days to think about it you decide you agree with the rest of the team, you can simply call the IEP coordinator and arrange to give your written permission.

Coming to a Consensus

IDEA doesn't specifically say how a team must come to a consensus; it just says that the team must be in agreement. It's not common to see an IEP team take a poll or a vote to see who is in agreement about the components of an IEP. Most teams will try to come to a consensus through conversation and discussion. It's your job to make it clear to school personnel when you're not in agreement by clearly saying either "I don't agree with that decision" or "I object to that being added to the IEP." To the best extent possible, make your reasons for objection clear and ask that they be noted in the narrative (or notes) section of the IEP.

You may be asked what you would recommend instead. If you don't have an alternative, it's okay to say so and ask that the team have a conversation about other service or program options. Just because you don't agree with something doesn't mean it is solely your responsibility to come up with a different plan.

Remember Your Rights

No matter how pressured you feel to agree with the plan, you have the right to disagree and to say so. You also have the right to make sure your disagreement is documented. More importantly, you have the right to refuse to sign the IEP or any other document on the spot. It is not a good idea to sign an IEP or evaluation form that is not completely filled out. No matter how much you trust the teachers or school personnel you are working with, you cannot be sure that what you have agreed to will be added to or deleted from the paperwork unless you see it. Ask to take the IEP home to look at it more carefully before signing or for the completed form to be mailed to you for your signature.

If you do decide to sign the form at the meeting, be sure to read it thoroughly before signing. Make sure it fairly represents the discussion of the IEP team, all the points that were brought up, and all the options that were considered. A good rule of thumb is to look at the form you are signing as if you were not a participant in the meeting. Someone who wasn't present should be able to read the form and from the level of performance, goals, and narrative be able to put together exactly what happened at the meeting.

It's Not All or Nothing

It's also good to keep in mind that an IEP is not an all-or-nothing process. You may not come to a consensus on every issue, but that doesn't mean you can't come to agreement on some of them. For example, if you and the school agree on your child's goals, placement, and services, but disagree on how much time is needed per week for one of the services, you don't have to turn down the entire IEP. In fact, it's better to agree to a once-weekly session of physical therapy, for instance, while making a clear note of the fact that you think your child needs an additional session per week. That way while you are negotiating with the school district (or filing a complaint), your child will at least get some of the service you and the school agree he needs.

Should you decide to accept an IEP in part, you'll need to make it very clear in writing what you are agreeing to and what you disagree with. You do this in two ways: by not checking off the box that says you approve of the IEP, and by adding a parent addendum. More specifically, if your school district's IEP form has a box before the signature line that indicates partial approval, check that off. If it doesn't have such a box, write "Partial approval only, see parent addendum for more information" above or next to your signature on the form. You'll want it to be written close to your signature so it doesn't get detached from the IEP form or overlooked.

QUESTION

Can I change my mind after giving permission for my child's IEP?
If you decide you don't want your child to be in a particular program or receive a service, you can revoke your consent by putting it in writing. There is a sample Revocation of Consent letter in Appendix B for your convenience.

Some IEP forms have a parent addendum page for you to add comments after your signature, but not all do. If there isn't one, you'll have to write one up and add it. There is a sample Parent Addendum form in Appendix C for your convenience. Be sure to clearly state your points of disagreement on the form. For example:

We have the following concerns about the IEP recommendations, document, discussion, or evaluations considered at this meeting:

We agree with all of the IEP except for the once-weekly session of physical therapy. It is our belief, as supported by the physical therapy evaluation report and recommendations, that our child needs an additional two sessions per week in order to benefit from his education.

What's Best for Your Child?

Hopefully, the decision to accept an IEP as written or ask for changes isn't a difficult one. After careful discussion, most IEP teams can come to a consensus on a program that—if not perfect—will at least provide your child with the assistance he needs to learn. It's often in the best interest of your child to provide at least partial approval to get special education services started.

Unfortunately, in some cases the program and services the school is offering isn't what's best for your child. If after careful thought you feel that your child's needs won't be adequately addressed by the plan proposed by the IEP team, you have the right to disagree and not give permission to have it implemented. In that case, your options are to negotiate informally with the school, request mediation through your state's Department of Education, or file a due process complaint.

CHAPTER 20

When Problems Arise at School

Sometimes, despite all your best efforts to work with the school district and advocate for your child, problems will come up with the school concerning your child's education. The information in this chapter is designed to give you some idea of the processes involved and avenues to take when things don't go right with special education. It's not a substitute for advice from a special education lawyer, but it can give you some idea of your options and what to discuss with a lawyer.

What to Do When the IEP Isn't Being Followed

In the most extreme of circumstances, you and the school might not be able agree about your child's need for special education at all, his diagnosis, program, placement, or other really important issues. These are big issues, ones that can interfere with the process of getting an individualized education program in place for your child. Some issues may need to be addressed in legal proceedings known as "due process." There are other issues that can impact your child's education, too, but some might be able to be resolved another way before taking legal measures.

ESSENTIAL

Your due process rights are outlined in the *Parental Rights and Procedural Safeguards* booklet that is offered to you at every IEP meeting or sent with the prior written notice. If you don't have one in your records, ask the school for another copy.

In some cases, you may discover that your child's IEP isn't being followed. The IEP is a legal document, and the school district is obligated to implement it. That means that in addition to working on your child's goals, all the services, modifications, accommodations, and other pieces of the plan need to be put into place as well. The school cannot pick and choose which parts of the plan they will honor.

Consider, for example, a case in which your child has a learning disability that makes it hard for him to take written notes in class and still be able to focus on what the teacher is saying. A reasonable accommodation for the IEP team to put in your child's plan would be for the regular education teacher to provide a copy of notes or an outline for these types of lessons. It may also be decided that an appropriate modification is for your child's work to be graded as pass/fail instead of using a letter grade system. All of your child's teachers are obligated to do these things because the IEP team decided they were necessary for him to be able to benefit from his education. If your child starts bringing home Cs and Ds on his homework in one of his classes or struggles to study for a test because he can't read his own notes, you know the IEP isn't being followed.

Talk to the Teacher First

As tempting as it may be to immediately call the principal or IEP coordinator, a better first step is to request a meeting with the teacher who isn't following the IEP. If you are able to sit down face-to-face with the teacher, do that instead of trying to talk about it over the phone. That serves a few purposes. You can bring a copy of your child's IEP with you to go over with the teacher, and there's more likely to be a record of a meeting that happens in the school than a phone conversation. You may also be able get a better sense as to whether the teacher is refusing to follow your child's IEP or whether there's a genuine misunderstanding.

If you remember, special education plans are written yearly, so your child's plan may have followed him from one grade to the next. Although teachers should have access to all of their students' IEPs before the school year begins, it's possible that your child's teacher has not seen your child's IEP or is not aware of the accommodations and modifications that have been agreed upon. Some teachers are also not always aware that these things have to be done all the time or in the regular education classroom.

When you sit down with a teacher who is not following your child's IEP, the best way to start the conversation is just by asking whether the teacher knows your child has a special education plan. If the teacher was at an IEP meeting with you, then the question to ask is whether she's seen a copy of the finalized IEP. Present a copy of the IEP and explain what it is you are concerned about, pointing specifically to the pieces of the plan that are not being followed in the classroom. You're likely to get one of a few responses:

- The teacher genuinely didn't know about the accommodations and modifications that needed to be made and has no problem putting them into place.
- The teacher knew about the accommodations and modifications but doesn't agree with them or thinks they are too much work to put into place.
- The teacher thinks your child is doing fine most of the time without the accommodations or modifications and doesn't think it's necessary to put them into place.

Of these particular responses, only the first one is acceptable, although any response that ends with a teacher agreeing to fulfill your child's IEP is good. If you hear anything otherwise, it's time to speak with somebody else.

When a Teacher Refuses to Follow the IEP

Not having enough time or having too many other kids in the classroom aren't valid reasons for your child's teacher to not provide accommodations in the classroom. That doesn't mean those things aren't true, but when it comes to things your child really needs to learn, you can't compromise because you feel bad for the teacher. Your child's IEP should be followed as written, and the decision not to follow it in the classroom isn't one a teacher can make. Deciding not to address goals because your child is "doing so well" or "doesn't need that" is not up to a teacher or service provider, either. It's a team decision.

FACT

If your child has not been receiving the services outlined in his IEP, he may qualify for compensatory services. That means he will get extra service time to make up the progress he didn't make when the service wasn't being provided.

If after meeting with the teacher you do not get a satisfactory resolution, you have a few in-house options before you start thinking about legal action. The first is to call the case manager listed on your child's IEP. This is typically the special education teacher who is working with your child, or it could be another special education teacher in the school. It is the case manager's responsibility to keep an eye on your child's program and make sure everything is going smoothly. Realistically, if your child's case manager doesn't work with him directly and everything has been going well, she may only check in when it's time to provide progress reports or when a meeting is coming up. A phone call to alert the case manager that things are not going smoothly may be all it takes to get your child's plan back on track.

Dealing with Disputes

There are five basic ways to resolve issues with the school district. The first two are informal ways to come to an agreement: an IEP review meeting and a facilitated IEP review meeting.

IEP Review Meetings

When you don't get anywhere with your child's teacher or service provider and don't feel as though speaking to the case manager was helpful, the next step is to call an IEP review meeting. Parents have the right to request a meeting at any time for any reason. In this circumstance, the reason would be your concern that the plan isn't being followed as written. The purpose of the meeting is to review the IEP to make sure it's appropriate and to discuss why it is not being followed. A sample letter for requesting an IEP review meeting is provided in Appendix B.

Try to go into this meeting with an open mind. If a teacher is saying a goal isn't being addressed because your child has met it or an accommodation or modification isn't being provided because your child doesn't need it, that could be true. That's a situation in which the team might need to rework the plan to more accurately reflect your child's current needs.

On the other hand, it could be that the school district or teacher isn't willing to do what your child's plan outlines. That makes for a very different conversation at a meeting. That's a conversation that centers around what support the teacher may need to implement your child's plan, or one that ends with you letting the IEP team know that you will be exercising your right to file a complaint.

Facilitated IEP Meetings

Before you move to filing a complaint, it may be a good idea to check with your school district's special education department or school board to see if they have a provision for having a facilitated meeting. Not all school districts will provide you with this option because it is not mentioned by IDEA or listed in the procedural safeguards as a way to resolve disputes.

Nonetheless, some districts prefer using an impartial facilitator to address conflicts before resorting to formal and legal options.

In a facilitated IEP meeting, the facilitator is someone who is not part of the IEP team and is impartial. He does not represent the school's interests or the interest of the parents; his job is to help everybody communicate effectively. He will work to focus all participants on the issues that are preventing you from writing an individualized education program that is in the best interest of your child. Having a facilitated meeting can be very helpful to make sure that everybody's views are heard respectfully and that all the options for your child's education are carefully considered, but it's not a legal proceeding. Facilitated IEP meetings are also not required by IDEA. If your school district doesn't have someone who can facilitate a meeting or doesn't agree to your suggestion of an outside facilitator, you'll have to move forward with a more formal option of dispute resolution.

What Are Due Process Rights?

There are times when an IEP meeting isn't going to solve the issues you have with your child's school. For example, if a school isn't providing a service that is on your child's IEP or you and the school do not agree on appropriate goals, the type of classroom in which your child should be placed, or other key issues, having another meeting with the team that is deadlocked is a waste of time. That's when you need to consider exercising the due process rights given to you by IDEA.

Due process is the legal procedures outlined by IDEA as to how to resolve a conflict between parents and schools. You have the right to try to resolve disputes about identification (or eligibility), evaluation, educational placement, or the provision of a FAPE to your child. When you and the school cannot agree on one or more of these issues, you have the right to file a due process complaint, which can be resolved either through mediation or a due process hearing. You also have the right to file a state complaint when you think that your child's school district has not followed the legal requirements of IDEA.

Filing a State Complaint

A state complaint is slightly different than a due process complaint. A due process complaint is filed to try to find a solution to a factual conflict between parents and a school district. It can be filed either by parents or by the school district. Once a due process complaint is filed with your state's Department of Education, there are specific steps and timelines that need to be followed in order to try to come to a resolution. A due process complaint is about how your child's FAPE is (or is not) being provided.

A state complaint, on the other hand, is a letter to a state agency to report a violation of the law. A violation of the rights provided under IDEA means the complaint will be filed with your state's Department of Education. A violation of the rights provided under the Americans with Disabilities Act or Section 504 will be filed with the Office of Civil Rights. You can find the contact information for these agencies on the U.S. Department of Education's website at *www.ed.gov*.

Unlike a due process complaint, a state complaint can be filed by an organization. That means if you are working with an advocacy group or a disability rights center, they can file a complaint on your child's behalf.

FACT

Disability rights organizations often file complaints when a school district's violation of the law affects more than just one child. If you know your child is not the only one affected, encourage other parents to come forward as well. It can strengthen your case.

How to File a Complaint

The complaint you file has to be about something the school district has done—or not done—that violates what IDEA requires of them. Some examples of IDEA violations are:

- Not providing your child's records upon request
- Failing to stick to evaluation, eligibility, and IEP timelines
- Not holding an IEP meeting, whether it is an annual meeting or a requested meeting

- Refusing to allow you the chance to truly be your child's representative at an IEP meeting—that can mean refusing to let you bring a support person or advocate, not allowing you equal say, or intimidating you into not participating
- Not discussing all of the pieces of an IEP at a meeting or providing a prewritten, predetermined IEP for you to sign
- Failing or refusing to follow or implement your child's IEP
- Not giving you notice before changing your child's IEP

In order for your complaint to be considered, it has to be filed within a year of the violation. You also need to send a copy of the complaint to the school district as well as to the state agency. It's a good idea to send everything by certified mail to make sure you can prove the letters were received and the date on which they were received.

A Note about Manifest Determination

There is another circumstance about which you can file a complaint: when you feel that the school district has suspended or expelled your child from school without going through the necessary procedures for a child in special education. These procedures, known as a manifestation determination review (MDR), are complex and can be confusing. The process begins if your child's behavior causes him to be suspended for more than ten days or expelled from school. After ten days, it can be considered to be a change in program placement. A change in placement for a child in special education is supposed to be a decision of the IEP team. Because of this, disciplinary action of this type requires a review to see if the discipline problem was caused by your child's disability or by the school district's failure to follow your child's IEP. Your child's records and IEP will be examined, and the team must answer the following questions:

1. Was your child's behavior directly caused by or related to his disability?
2. Was your child's behavior a direct result of the school's failure to create an individualized education program that met his needs, or to implement one that did?

If both questions can be answered no, then your child's behavior is not considered to be a manifestation of his disability and the change in placement can happen. If either of the questions can be answered yes, then the behavior is a manifestation of your child's disability. When the latter is the case, the IEP team is required by law to do a functional behavior assessment of your child and create a behavior intervention plan (BIP). Or, if your child has a BIP that wasn't being followed or needs to be changed, the team has to make changes that will help it better meet your child's needs.

ALERT

A manifestation determination review is a serious matter and involves very complicated legal issues. Consulting an attorney who specializes in special education law is highly advised.

Once an assessment is complete and an appropriate behavior plan created, in most cases your child can return to her previous placement with those changes put into place. There are exceptions to the manifestation determination ten-day rule. If your child has been suspended or expelled for something involving weapons, drugs, or serious injury, your child can be removed from her current placement for up to forty-five days without your agreement and without a hearing.

What to Say in a Complaint

Your state may have a form to use, so before you write a complaint letter, use the U.S. Department of Education website's state contact page (*www2 .ed.gov/about/contacts/state/index.html*) to find your state's Department of Education contact information. Even if there isn't a form for you to follow, you will be given the address to which to send your complaint letter and probably the name of the person to contact. Your complaint letter should include your name, address, and other contact information; your child's full name; the school and district; a detailed description of the violation or violations; what type of resolution you are looking for; and your signature. That description should include the date, location, time, and as much specific information you can provide. A sample letter can be found in Appendix B. Here's what that letter might look like:

Jane Doe
Compliance Unit
Special Education Division
Department of Education
City, State, ZIP Code

Dear Ms. Doe:

I am formally requesting an investigation into legal violations by the Local School District, located at Main Street, in Anywhere, Anystate. I am requesting this pursuant to state law and IDEA, which provides me the right to file such a complaint if I feel the district is in violation of IDEA. It is my assertion that the district violated the timeline in which to evaluate and hold an eligibility meeting for my child. The details of my complaint are as follow:

On October 1, 2014, I requested and signed a referral for evaluation for special education services for my child, at which time I was informed I would receive an evaluation plan within fifteen school days. I did not receive such an evaluation plan until October 31, 2014. When I signed and returned the form the following day, I was told that the evaluation would be scheduled "after the new year" and we would meet sometime in February to discuss my child's eligibility for special education services. In doing so, the school district violated Part B of IDEA, which provides for an evaluation plan to be provided within fifteen days of receipt of a written referral. Furthermore, in waiting until early 2015 to evaluate and hold an eligibility meeting, the district has violated the timeline that provides for sixty days to evaluate and hold a meeting after parental consent to evaluate is received.

I am requesting that the evaluation be completed within fifteen days of the conclusion of your investigation and that an eligibility meeting be held within thirty days. I also am requesting reimbursement for the legal fees I have incurred in trying to address the school's failure to adhere to its obligations under IDEA.

I look forward to confirmation that you have received this complaint and meeting with your investigator.

Respectfully,
Ima Y.
(555)-555-5555

What Happens after You File a Complaint

Once you file a complaint with the state Department of Education, there must be an investigation and a decision has to be made on the issue within sixty days of receiving the complaint. This time may be extended if there are "exceptional circumstances" in regard to the complaint or if you and the school district go to mediation to try to solve the problem. You will be given the chance to provide more information about your complaint, and an investigator will meet with the school district to hear its side and review records.

Mediation

Another option for dealing with disputes is to go to mediation. Mediation is a formal and legal step that either a parent or a school district can request through the state's education department. You must file a request for mediation with the state Department of Education and provide a copy of the request to the school district. For your convenience, a sample Request for Mediation letter is provided in Appendix B, as is a sample letter to request a due process hearing.

Mediation is a way to try to resolve things prior to going before a hearing officer. It is voluntary, meaning the school district cannot force you to sit down with a mediator before you file for a due process hearing. But that also means the school district can refuse to sit in mediation with you and effectively force you to request a due process hearing.

Mediation versus Due Process Hearing

In a mediation session, you will meet with a representative of the school district and a neutral party appointed by the state. That person is there to help you come to an agreement, but, unlike a hearing officer, the neutral party doesn't have the power to make decisions. He will work with you and the school to come to a compromise. In mediation you will sit down and talk over the situation, while a due process hearing is a legal proceeding in which each side puts on a case and the officer makes a decision.

Once you file for due process, whether you're asking specifically for mediation or a hearing, the school district has to schedule a "resolution session." This meeting has to take place within fifteen days of the district's receipt of the notice that you're filing for due process.

FACT

IDEA does not require a resolution meeting if the school district is the party that files for a due process hearing.

The point of a resolution meeting is to make one last effort to try to come to an agreement before the formal process gets underway. Any agreement that you come to has to be signed by you and the school and can be enforced by the court system. Technically, you have the right to waive this meeting, but the school district has to agree to waive it, too. If they don't and you decide not to participate, it's possible that the Department of Education will dismiss your case and not hold mediation or a due process hearing.

The "Stay Put" Rule

When you are in formal negotiations with the school district about some element of your child's IEP—whether the negotiation is the initial resolution meeting, mediation, or a due process hearing—your child may be subject to the "stay put" rule. This rule stops everything right where it is. Your child stays in his current educational placement and program until a formal agreement has been reached or a court decision has been made. "Stay put" can work either to your advantage or your disadvantage.

If you are in conflict with the school district's desire to place your child outside the regular education classroom, she will remain in the regular education classroom until the conflict is resolved. This can be beneficial if it's what you wanted anyway because your child is where you want her to be and because it continues to provide information and evidence of how she is able to perform in the regular education classroom. On the other hand, if you want your child to be placed in a different program and the school doesn't agree, she will remain in her current program until a resolution is reached. This may not be to your child's advantage, especially since the process may take a long time and she is not benefitting from her current program.

The Advantages of Mediation

Trying mediation before taking your dispute to a hearing has some advantages. It gives you a chance to get a better idea of the reasoning behind the school's position, which can make it easier to find a compromise. You may also find that the school district is more willing to make some concessions once it knows you are willing to take your case to hearing. Going to a due process hearing can be expensive and time-consuming, and it brings unwanted exposure to a school district. By the same token, it almost certainly means you and the district will not have a cordial relationship moving forward, something that can be difficult once the dispute is resolved. Mediation is a less adversarial way of dealing with a dispute and allows both parties to still have some say in what happens.

QUESTION

What do I do if I realize at mediation that I don't have a strong case?
Mediation is a good time to find this out. It gives you a chance to rethink your position, figure out what's going to benefit your child, and come to an agreement with the school district without the chance of a hearing officer dismissing your case.

Mediation is also less expensive for you. You may choose to have a lawyer or advocate present, but you don't have to, and the school district can only bring their lawyer if you bring one. Mediation also gives you a chance to see the strengths and weaknesses of both sides of the dispute, and if you don't come to an agreement, you have not given up your right to take the dispute to hearing.

The Disadvantages of Mediation

Mediation also has its downsides. Since the whole idea behind mediation is to come to a compromise that both sides are willing to accept, you are unlikely to get everything you want for your child—you'll probably have to settle for something else. And if mediation is unsuccessful, you end up going through everything all over again at a due process hearing, which not only makes it longer before your child's FAPE is decided, but it also can increase expenses and stress.

What Happens in Mediation

Mediation experiences differ from family to family, but the basic process is the same. The mediator will choose a convenient time and place for you to sit down with representatives from the school district. Typically, the representatives are the special education director and someone else who is familiar with your child and her program. A mediation session isn't time limited, so it can take anywhere from a few hours to an entire day to spanning across multiple days. However, if you haven't reached an agreement by the end of an entire day's worth of negotiation, it's fairly likely your next step will be a due process hearing.

Just like an IEP meeting, the session begins with introductions, and the mediator will briefly explain why you're all there and what the rules of mediation are. You then have a chance to make an opening statement to explain your side of the conflict. You should do so as clearly as possible, explaining what the issue or issues are as you see it, why you're in disagreement with the school district, and what you'd like to see happen. You don't have to be unemotional—there's nothing wrong with expressing your feelings—but stay cordial and don't verbally attack the school or its representatives. Your statement should also include any concerns you have about legal violations, even if you've filed a state complaint about them.

The next step is for the school district to make its opening statement. The representative may try to refute what you've said or be defensive and impolite, but try to keep your cool and simply take notes of what is being said. Those notes will come in handy in the next part of the mediation process. You and the school representatives will each have a chance to meet privately with the mediator, who is not able to share anything you say unless you give your permission. That gives you the chance to speak as openly and honestly as you want or need to. The mediator will try to clarify the issues, get an idea of how each side wants to resolve the situation, and go back and forth between you and the school representative.

In the best of circumstances, things are clarified and you are able to get a sense of what the school's bottom line is. The session can end in one of four ways: a complete settlement of all the issues, a partial settlement (agreeing on some issues and not others), no agreement on issues but an agreement to try mediation again, or no agreement on issues and no plan to continue mediation. If you do come to a settlement, the mediator will fill out a form that details what has been agreed to, what is still up in the air, and what will happen next. In some cases, the next step will be to write the IEP according to the settled-upon terms, but in others the next step will be to go to a due process hearing.

Filing Due Process

When you and the school district are unable (or unwilling) to come to a resolution in another way, the only available option that is left is to have a due process hearing. You can only file a complaint within two years of knowing of the issue. It's worded that way because there are some cases in which a parent does not find out about a failure to provide a service or inaccuracies in the IEP record until after the fact. In most cases, though, if there's something you and the school are in conflict over, you'll know about it sooner rather than later.

If you have already gone through the mediation process unsuccessfully, you have already begun due process. However, you will need to formally file a request for a hearing, either using the form provided by your state's education department or by writing a letter. IDEA outlines some very specific things that need to be included in your letter. They are:

1. Your name and address (if you have shared custody of your child, provide both parents' names and addresses)

2. Your child's name and address
3. The name of your child's school and school district
4. A detailed description of the issue or issues in dispute
5. How you would like to see the issue(s) resolved
6. Whether you are requesting mediation or a hearing

QUESTION

Can a school district file a due process complaint against a parent? A school district has the right to file a due process complaint just as a parent does. It's not as common, but there are situations in which a district feels that the issue at dispute is important enough to take before a hearing officer.

It is very important to provide as much detail as possible and include every issue that is causing conflict. At a hearing, you can only discuss and present evidence about the issues that are noted in the complaint. During a hearing, both sides have an opportunity to present witness testimony, documents, and legal arguments to the hearing officer. If you are looking at going to a hearing, having a lawyer is absolutely in your best interest. The hearing is a legal proceeding and the hearing officer's decision is legally binding.

Your Rights and Responsibilities

Both you and the school district have rights and responsibilities when it comes to due process hearings. You have the right to hire a lawyer or enlist a specially trained advocate, but you will need to foot the expense. If you win the hearing, the school district has to reimburse those fees. At least five days before the hearing, you and the district both have to give each other evaluations and evaluation reports that will be considered at the hearing.

You also have the right to request that a hearing is either closed or open to the public. You and your lawyer can talk about which option would be best for your case. Sometimes having a hearing open to the press and public can be to your advantage, but it also means your family's privacy will be compromised. You also have the right to have your child at the hearing if you want. It's important to consider the effect hearing all the testimony and evidence might have on your child, both in terms of his emotional state and his ability to be comfortable in school in the future.

Finally, you also have the rights to obtain a recording of the hearing, to receive a written decision after the hearing, and to appeal to the court system if you do not agree with the decision.

The Advantages and Disadvantages of a Due Process Hearing

Going to a hearing is a tough process. It takes a lot of time and emotional and financial resources, but sometimes it's the only way to make sure your child gets the education he needs. It's very important to weigh whether you are fighting for what your child needs or for a different reason. IDEA 2004 added a clause that allows hearing officers to order parents to pay the school district's legal fees if you have filed due process for "improper purposes," such as to harass the school district into a settlement, to cause deliberate delays to take advantage of the stay put rule, or to try to get unreasonable or unnecessary services for your child. If you are going to due process for the right reasons, you needn't worry about this clause. If you win, not only will your attorney fees be reimbursed, but your child will also get the education he needs.

The Due Process Hearing

A due process hearing proceeds much like a court case. After a due process complaint is filed, the party who did not file the complaint has fifteen days to notify the hearing officer in writing if they think the complaint doesn't meet the due process requirements under IDEA. The hearing officer will then decide within five days if the hearing will move forward.

Your lawyer and the school district's lawyer will have to subpoena and prepare witnesses, including evaluators, service providers, teachers, you, and possibly even your child. Everybody has to provide a list of all the written evidence that should be considered at the hearing. At the hearing, once the tape recorder is turned on, everybody is introduced. You or your lawyer will make an opening statement, the school district will make an opening statement, and then you will each present your witnesses. After all the witnesses have been questioned and cross-examined, each side will have a chance to clear up issues or statements that came up during testimony and then give a closing statement. As an alternative to a closing statement, each party can choose to submit a written summary (or brief) that sums up its position and highlights the evidence, law, or witness testimony that supports that position.

What Happens after a Due Process Hearing

After the hearing, the hearing officer will provide a written decision that addresses all the issues and states whether your child received or was denied a free appropriate public education. The decision has to be issued within forty-five days, but the clock starts only after a resolution meeting was waived or mediation ended with a written statement saying no agreement was reached. The hearing officer's decision can be appealed, but how that is handled differs from state to state. What is the same across the board is that unless an appeal is filed within the time frame specified by your state, the hearing officer's decision is final.

Your Child's Unique Needs

When your child shows signs of a disability that affects her learning, a due process hearing probably isn't even on your radar. For most parents, it is never a part of the special education experience, and hopefully it will not be part of yours, either. You may have some difficulty negotiating and understanding the special education system, but the more informed you are, the better the chances are that you will be able to successfully advocate for your child. When you know what is next in the process and are prepared to ask questions to be a vocal and active member of your child's IEP team, you are taking on the challenge of helping make sure your child has a successful learning experience.

As you negotiate the system, keep in mind that what you are trying to do is make sure your child's unique needs are met so she can learn, have positive interactions with her peers, and be prepared for life after school. Keep in mind, too, that IDEA is on your side. Remember, that's what special education is for: to meet the unique needs of children with disabilities.

APPENDIX A

An Online Sample IEP

Every school district has its own IEP form, although some states have created forms that all school districts in that state must use. All the forms must have the information required by IDEA, but there is no requirement as to what the form must look like. It's a good idea to ask your school district for a copy of the IEP form it uses as a way to familiarize yourself with the specifics of what will be included on your child's IEP. In order to give you an idea of what an IEP form can look like, the sample form used and created by the Maine Department of Education can be found at *www.maine.gov/doe/specialed/forms/index.html*. This IEP form is considered a model form and is public domain material. The form that is used where you live can be found on your state's Department of Education website.

Sample Letters

Following are sample letters that will come in handy at different points in the special education process. Replace the underlined items with your specific details, and fill in the italicized options where appropriate.

Sample Letter: Request for Information about the Special Education Referral Process

Your name
Your address
City, State, ZIP Code
Phone number

Today's date
Principal's name
Name of school
Street address
City, State, ZIP Code
cc: child's teacher's name, child's name education record
Dear principal's name,

I am writing you in regard to my child, child's full name, who is having difficulty in school. I have spoken with the teacher, teacher's name, in regard to my concerns. I know that there is a specific process to follow in order to initiate a referral for evaluation for special education services and would like to know more about how that process works. I am requesting that you please send me information about the process and how I can initiate a referral for evaluation.

Thank you for your assistance. I look forward to learning more about the special education referral process.

Should you have any questions, I can be reached at the above number.

Sincerely,
Your name

Sample Letter: Request for a 504 Plan Meeting

Your name
Your address
City, State, ZIP Code
Phone number

Today's date
Principal's name
Name of school

Street address

City, State, ZIP Code

Dear principal's name,

We are writing to formally request a meeting to create a 504 plan for our child, child's name. Child's name has [*describe condition*] that impacts daily functioning in school.

Enclosed you will find documentation from [*list doctor's or therapist's name, or leave this paragraph out if you don't have any documentation*]. We will also bring a copy of this documentation to the meeting with us. Please let us know if you require any further information prior to meeting.

We have spoken with our child's teacher, teacher's name, about our intent to request this meeting. In order to make sure a plan can be developed and appropriate accommodations implemented in a timely manner, we would like to have this meeting as soon as possible.

Please let us know of the soonest meeting times and dates at which all of the necessary school personnel can attend.

We look forward to hearing from you within the next week about the request for a meeting.

Thank you for your help.

Sincerely,

Your name

Enclosure: [*whatever documentation you provide*]

Sample Letter: Request for Educational Records

Your name

Your address

City, State, ZIP Code

Phone number

Today's date

Principal's name

Name of school

Street address

City, State, ZIP Code

Re: request and parental consent for student's education records

Dear principal's name,

I am writing to request a copy of all school records pertaining to my child, <u>child's name and birthdate</u>. I am requesting all education records that the school district has in relation to my child, no matter the location of these records within the school district, i.e., the special education office, central office, local school, or any other office or department. As provided for by §300.616 of the Individuals with Disabilities Education Improvement Act of 2004, I am also requesting a list of the "types and locations" of said education records.

This request is made under the provisions of the Family Educational Records and Privacy Act and IDEA 2004 and includes all records that contain personally identifiable information about <u>child's first name</u> and us, <u>parent's names</u>, using all identifiers the school district employs.

Included in this request are all tests, report cards, progress reports, incident reports, and teacher and staff notes regarding my child including interoffice correspondence, communication log notes, meeting notes, observations, evaluations, notices for meetings, current and previous IEPs and 504 plans, and any records in any format not stated that pertain to my child.

I would really appreciate having these records within five days of your receipt of this letter. I will call you on <u>three days after anticipated receipt of letter</u> to make arrangements for picking up and/or copying these records.

Please feel free to contact me if you have questions. Thank you for your help.

Respectfully,
<u>Your name</u>

Sample Letter: Request to Begin the Special Education and Evaluation Process

<u>Your name</u>
<u>Your address</u>
<u>City, State, ZIP Code</u>
<u>Phone number</u>

<u>Today's date</u>
<u>Principal's or school's special education administrator's name</u>
<u>Name of school</u>

Street address

City, State, ZIP Code

Dear principal's or special education administrator's name,

I am writing to formally request that my child, child's full name, be evaluated for special education services under the Child Find obligations of the Individuals with Disabilities Act (IDEA). I am asking that s/he be given a comprehensive educational assessment by the school district in regard to the concerns I have outlined below. I am also requesting that an IEP meeting be scheduled to discuss an evaluation and assessment plan that will be most appropriate to look at child's name needs.

As part of this assessment process and conversation, I also would like to request that child's name be assessed under Section 504 of the Rehabilitation Act of 1973 to see whether s/he has a disability as defined by that law, and to identify what accommodations are needed in the general education classroom in the event s/he is not found eligible for special education services. For that reason, I would ask that the 504 coordinator be present at this initial meeting as well. Please note that I am not saying that I am comfortable substituting a 504 assessment for a special education assessment, only that I think both are an appropriate way to determine child's name needs and disability.

I am concerned that s/he is struggling in school and may need special education support to learn. Child's name is in grade level at school name in teacher's name class. More specifically, I am concerned that s/he is not learning to read as easily as his/her peers. S/he struggles with [*explain your concerns in detail, using evidence to back it up if you have it*]. I have spoken with teacher's name on date of conference to discuss these concerns and the following has been tried to help:

[*Describe any interventions tried by you or the school*]

Please feel free to call me for more information. I will follow up with you on date three days after this letter will be received.

Respectfully,

Your name

Sample Letter: Request to Modify/Change Educational Records

Your name
Your address
City, State, ZIP Code
Phone number

Today's date
Special education administrator's name
Name of school
Street address
City, State, ZIP Code
cc: Superintendent's name, child's name education record
Re: child's full name and full birthdate
Dear special education administrator's name,

Recently, I received and reviewed a copy of my child's education records. I know that under IDEA I have the right to request amendment to any inaccurate or misleading information or information that violates my child's privacy. I would like to exercise that right and request the following portions or files be amended, for the following reasons:

[*List each document, the information you take issue with, why you think it is wrong, and what you want changed*]

As stated, I believe the information to be inaccurate, misleading, or a violation of child's name's privacy, and I request that the education record be changed immediately to fix this situation.

I look forward to seeing your written decision on this matter. Thank you.
Respectfully,
Your name

Sample Letter: Reject Evaluation Plan

Your name
Your address
City, State, ZIP Code
Phone number

Today's date

<u>IEP coordinator's name</u>
<u>Name of school</u>
<u>Street address</u>
<u>City, State, ZIP Code</u>
cc: <u>principal's name</u>, <u>child's name</u> education record
Dear <u>IEP coordinator's name</u>,

I am writing in regard to the proposed special education evaluation plan for my child, <u>child's full name</u>, which I received on <u>date received</u>. I have examined the plan in detail, and I am rejecting the proposed plan for the following reasons:

[*Choose appropriate reasons or add your own*]

- I do not believe the proposed testing reflects the concerns that have been raised in regard to my child's performance in school.
- I do not feel the selected evaluator has the appropriate credentials or experience evaluating children with <u>child's name</u>'s disability.

I would like to meet with you in regard to creating a more appropriate evaluation plan as I still believe moving forward with an evaluation is appropriate. I am available to meet about this matter at your convenience.

I look forward to hearing from you in the next week.

Respectfully,
<u>Your name</u>

Sample Letter: Accept Evaluation Plan with Conditions

<u>Your name</u>
<u>Your address</u>
<u>City, State, ZIP Code</u>
<u>Phone number</u>

<u>Today's date</u>
<u>IEP coordinator's name</u>
<u>Name of school</u>
<u>Street address</u>

City, State, ZIP Code

cc: principal's name, child's name education record

Dear IEP coordinator's name,

I am writing in regard to the proposed special education evaluation plan for my child, child's full name, which I received on date received. I have examined the plan in detail and am prepared to accept the plan conditionally.

While I am in agreement that [*list tests for which you are giving permission*] would be helpful in determining the presence of a disability, I do not feel that the plan proposes to evaluate every area of suspected disability.

I believe additional testing is needed in the area of [*list area you think needs to be looked at and reasons why*]. I am formally requesting that [*specific tests or type of testing*] be added to the evaluation plan.

Furthermore, after some investigation, I do not feel that the tests on the list (other than those I have mentioned) will provide reliable information and do not give my permission for them to be administered.

I look forward to hearing from you in the next week as to how you wish to proceed. I am available to meet about this matter at your convenience.

Respectfully,

Your name

Sample Letter: Request for a Joint Eligibility/ IEP Meeting

Your name
Your address
City, State, ZIP Code
Phone number

Today's date
IEP coordinator's name
Name of school
Street address
City, State, ZIP Code

cc: child's teacher's name, principal's name, child's name education record

Re: <u>child's full name and full birthdate</u>

Dear <u>IEP coordinator's name</u>,

After reviewing the evaluation reports and other information pertaining to my child's evaluation for special education services, I think there is enough information for us to talk about eligibility and discuss the details of an IEP at the same meeting. In order to make scheduling easier for all, I would appreciate it if you would set aside enough time to discuss both items at the IEP meeting scheduled for <u>meeting date and time.</u> [*You can omit the end of this sentence if a meeting has not yet been scheduled.*]

I would also appreciate the opportunity to review all reports and other written material that will be introduced by the school at the IEP meeting, preferably at least two weeks prior to the meeting.

Thank you for your assistance. I look forward to hearing from you.

Respectfully,

<u>Your name</u>

Sample Letter: Request to Visit Programs

<u>Your name</u>
<u>Your address</u>
<u>City, State, ZIP Code</u>
<u>Phone number</u>

<u>Today's date</u>
<u>IEP coordinator's name</u>
<u>Name of school</u>
<u>Street address</u>
<u>City, State, ZIP Code</u>
cc: <u>principal of the school with program</u>
Re: <u>child's full name and birthdate</u>

Dear <u>IEP coordinator's name</u>,

I am writing to you to seek permission to visit programs that may be looked at as appropriate placements for my child, <u>child's name</u>, in the future.

I am aware that placement decisions can only be made by the IEP team at or after an IEP meeting has been held, but in order to be an informed and effective decision-making member of the team, it would be helpful for me to see the available programs. I also understand that in providing me with names of programs and granting me permission to visit you are not rendering an opinion as to whether these programs are the appropriate placement for my child.

Please know that I will follow any policies that exist in regard to parental visitation. Thank you for your help in this matter. I look forward to hearing from you.

Respectfully,

Your name

Sample Letter: Request for Prior Written Notice

Your name
Your address
City, State, ZIP Code
Phone number

Today's date
IEP coordinator's name
Name of school
Street address
City, State, ZIP Code
cc: principal's name, child's name education record
Dear IEP coordinator's name,

At our [*meeting, phone call, conversation*] on date of contact, we discussed my child, child's name, [*evaluation, program placement, IEP, services, etc.*]. I asked that [*action to be taken*] or was told that the school [*action proposed or denied*].

I have not received this information in writing, and I am respectfully requesting that I receive prior written notice as provided for by IDEA, at 34 CRF §300.503. More specifically, I am requesting that I receive notice of [*list the decisions, actions, meetings, program changes, etc. about which you would like full documentation and explanations*].

I look forward to seeing a detailed prior written notice as soon as possible.

Thank you.

Respectfully,

Your name

Sample Letter: Request an Independent Evaluation at Public Expense

Your name
Your address
City, State, ZIP Code
Phone number

Today's date
Special education administrator's name
Name of school
Street address
City, State, ZIP Code
cc: principal's name, child's name education record
Dear special education administrator's name,

My child, child's name, is in the grade level at name of school. S/he has recently been evaluated for special education services by the school district's evaluator, name of evaluator. I received the evaluation reports and am requesting an independent educational evaluation for my child. I understand that IDEA provides for an independent evaluation at public expense. I am requesting this independent evaluation based on the following reasons:

[*List your reasons in detail with supporting quotes or data as necessary*]

I am requesting that my child be evaluated in the following areas:

[*List areas in which IEE is requested*]

I plan to have name of evaluator, of name center/hospital/or other affiliation, conduct the evaluation. Please contact his/her office at independent evaluator's phone number to arrange payment for these services.

I understand that unless the school district can prove at a due process hearing that the current evaluation is comprehensive, the school is responsible for the cost of the independent evaluation. If I have not heard from you in writing within 5 days or your receipt of this letter regarding whether you intend to request a hearing on this issue, I will assume that the school district intends to honor the request for an independent educational evaluation at public expense.

I also am aware that since the evaluation will be done at public expense, it must be comparable to that done by the school district's evaluator. Please contact name of evaluator's office to discuss the criteria and conditions, and to provide information about to whom the evaluation report should be sent for consideration by the IEP team.

Thank you and I look forward to hearing from you about this request.

Respectfully,

<u>Your name</u>

Sample Letter: Objection to a Specific IEP Participant

<u>Your name</u>
<u>Your address</u>
<u>City, State, ZIP Code</u>
<u>Phone number</u>

<u>Today's date</u>
<u>IEP coordinator's name</u>
<u>Name of school</u>
<u>Street address</u>
<u>City, State, ZIP Code</u>
cc: <u>principal's name</u>, <u>child's name</u> education record
Dear <u>IEP coordinator's name</u>,

I have received my prior written notice in regard to <u>child's name</u> IEP meeting <u>on meeting date.</u> I understand that <u>name of participant you have an objection to</u> will be attending this meeting. As far as I am aware, <u>participant's name</u> has no knowledge of my child or any information that could be helpful to the IEP team.

Therefore, I am formally requesting that <u>s/he</u> does not attend <u>child's name</u>'s IEP meeting unless you can provide a specific reason as to why <u>participant's name</u>'s presence is necessary to develop/review an IEP.

Should you not provide a reason and insist that <u>participant's name</u> attend this meaning, I will take the more formal step of filing a written complaint with the school district and the Department of Education.

I look forward to hearing from you in regard to this matter.

Respectfully,

<u>Your name</u>

Sample Letter: Revocation of Parental Consent for Special Education Programs and Services

Your name
Your address
City, State, ZIP Code
Phone number

Today's date
IEP coordinator's name
Name of school
Street address
City, State, ZIP Code
cc: principal's name, child's name's education record
Dear IEP coordinator's name,

I am the parent of child's name who is a grade level student at school's name. I am aware that an IEP team determined my child is eligible for special education services under the category of category of IEP eligibility and that I provided my consent for special education and related services. At this time, I wish to formally revoke my consent for the following services:

[List the services for which you are revoking your consent.]

I am aware that school district's name will provide me with prior written notice outlining when the revoked services will end and that these services will stop being provided to my child within a reasonable time frame of your receipt of this written notice of revocation of parental consent for service.

I am further aware that my revocation of the above services does not mean I am waiving my child's right to be evaluated or receive special education services in the future, that all future requests for evaluation will be considered a new referral for evaluation, and that my request to revoke services does not mean the school district is required to remove reference of receipt of special education services from my child's education record.

Please feel free to contact me if you have questions. Thank you for your prompt attention to this matter.

Respectfully,
Your name

Sample Letter: Request for an IEP Review Meeting

<u>Your name</u>
<u>Your address</u>
<u>City, State, ZIP Code</u>
<u>Phone number</u>

<u>Today's date</u>
<u>IEP coordinator's name</u>
<u>Name of school</u>
<u>Street address</u>
<u>City, State, ZIP Code</u>
cc: <u>principal's name</u>, <u>child's name</u> education record
Re: <u>child's full name and full birthdate</u>
Dear <u>IEP coordinator's name</u>,

I am writing to formally request that an IEP review meeting be scheduled to discuss <u>child's name</u>'s IEP. More specifically, I would like to discuss [*explain briefly why you think the team needs to meet or what your concerns are*].

In addition to the team members who, under law, are required to attend the meeting, I would also like to request that <u>participant's name</u> be present. [*If there are specific people who work with your child, have evaluated your child, or whom you think are otherwise critical to this meeting, add their names.*]

I will be accompanied by <u>educational advocate's name or attorney's name</u>. [*This is the time to let the school know whether or not you will be bringing an educational advocate or attorney with you. If not, you can omit this line.*]

Please contact me if you have questions. I look forward to hearing from you about this matter.

Respectfully,
<u>Your name</u>

Sample Letter: Complaint Letter

<u>Compliance officer's name</u>
Compliance Unit
Special Education Division
<u>Your state</u> Department of Education
City, State, ZIP Code

Dear <u>compliance officer's name</u>:

I am formally requesting an investigation into legal violations by the <u>name of your local school district</u>, located at <u>street address</u>, in <u>town/city, state</u>. I am requesting this pursuant to state law and IDEA, which provides me the right to file such a complaint if I feel the district is in violation of IDEA. It is my assertion that the district [*describe violation(s)*]. The details of my complaint are as follow:

[*Provide specific date(s) on which violation(s) occurred, and cite the specific right that was violated if you can.*]

I am requesting that [*describe the specific measures you want the school district to take*].

I look forward to confirmation that you have received this complaint and meeting with your investigator.

Respectfully,

<u>Your name</u>

<u>Your phone number</u>

Sample Letter: Request for Mediation

<u>Your name</u>
<u>Your address</u>
<u>City, State, ZIP Code</u>
<u>Phone number</u>

<u>Today's date</u>
<u>Your state</u> Department of Education
<u>Street address</u>
<u>City, State, ZIP Code</u>

I am the parent of <u>child's full name</u>, who is a student receiving special education services from <u>school district's name</u> at <u>school name</u>. I am writing to formally request mediation of a dispute between myself and the school district with regard to my child's education.

I would like to be able to resolve this dispute without having to take the matter to a due process hearing, which is why I am requesting mediation. The issues at hand are:

[*Explain the reasons you are in dispute with the school district, stating the facts and why and how you and the school district disagree.*]

I look forward to hearing from you in regard to setting up mediation.

Respectfully,

Your name

Sample Letter: Request a Due Process Hearing

Your name
Your address
City, State, ZIP Code
Phone number

Today's date
Superintendent's name
Name of school district
Street address
City, State, ZIP Code

cc: local education agency's name and address [*Your state's Department of Education*]

Dear superintendent's title and last name and your state's name Department of Education,

I am writing to formally request a due process hearing with an impartial hearing officer in regard to school district's failure to provide my child, child's full name, a free appropriate public education. My child, who resides at child's address, is a student who receives special education services at school's name.

My reasons for requesting this hearing are:

[*Explain in detail the reasons you want a hearing, making sure to stick to the facts and describing how you and the school disagree. Describe what it is the school wishes or does not wish to do and why you think this is a problem.*]

I think these problems can be resolved in the following ways:

[*Explain what you want and/or ways you think a solution can be reached.*]

Respectfully,

Your name

APPENDIX C

Sample Forms

Sample Form: Progress Chart

Write one IEP goal in each box. As you receive information as to how your child is progressing toward that goal, make note of the date and the information the school has provided for you. If you are seeing progress at home as well, you may also want to make note of that.

Goal:	Date of Report:	Progress Reported:

Goal:	Date of Report:	Progress Reported:

Goal:	Date of Report:	Progress Reported:

Sample Form: Goal Chart

Use your records binder to take notes on your child's present level of performance in the subject areas that are causing difficulty. Consider the improvement you'd like to see him make, take notes of the skills needed, and write a suggested goal based on that information.

Subject Area	PLOP	Skills to Work On	Suggested Goal

Sample Form: IEP Preparation Checklist

Once you have an idea of what you want your child's program to look like, you can start going through a checklist of the things that need to be part of your child's IEP. Here are some things to think about:

What Classroom Setting Is Best for My Child?

Think about the type or types of classroom you think would be most appropriate for your child. Check off all that apply and add your notes at the end.

- ◯ Regular education classroom with pull-out special education support
- ◯ Regular education classroom with in-class support
- ◯ Regular education classroom with accommodations
- ◯ Specific type of special education classroom (note the program below)
- ◯ Multiage classroom
- ◯ Classroom with same-age peers

Notes:

What Are My Child's Needs in Terms of Teachers/Staff?

Indicate the ideal staffing situation for your child's classroom.

- ◯ Small teacher-to-student ratio (no more than ____ students per teacher)
- ◯ Classroom aide
- ◯ One-to-one aide
- ◯ Special education teacher trained in teaching your child's specific disability
- ◯ Special education teacher
- ◯ Regular education teacher with special education support available

Notes:

How Does My Child Need to Be Taught?

Identify, if known, what types of teaching strategies and curriculum you would like to see implemented for your child.

- ◯ Applied behavioral analysis (ABA)
- ◯ Increased visual supports in teaching (i.e., picture schedules, visual directions)
- ◯ Sign language
- ◯ Braille or large print
- ◯ Specific curriculum or method of teaching (indicated in Notes)

Notes:

Which Related Services Does My Child Need?

- ○ Psychological services and/or counseling
- ○ Social work services
- ○ Occupational therapy services
- ○ Physical therapy services
- ○ Speech-language and audiology services
- ○ Orientation and mobility services
- ○ Special transportation
- ○ Interpreter services
- ○ Assistive technology
- ○ School nurse services

Notes (include information about amount of services and/or specific programs, as recommended by evaluators):

Is There an Existing Program That Fits My Child's Needs?

Note any programs (either in the school district or outside of it) that you think would be a good fit for your child:

What Goals Should My Child Be Working Toward?

Make note of the areas in which your child is having difficulty and need to be addressed by a special education program.

Are There Other Needs to Consider?

- ○ Health issues that involve staff training
- ○ Medication
- ○ Social needs
- ○ Special transportation
- ○ Transition planning
- ○ Life skills/vocational needs

Notes:

What Involvement Should My Child Have in the Regular Education Classroom?

○ Percentage of time/number of hours spent in the regular education classroom _____
○ Modifications needed
○ Accommodations for testing

Notes:

Sample Form: Program Visit Checklist

When you visit a potential program for your child, make sure to take notes about the program and what you learn about it. Use this checklist to help you keep track of the different programs and information you glean from your visit. If you are unable to fill it all in during the visit, try to find time to ask the teacher or administrator your remaining questions.

Date: _____

School visited: _____

Class or program name: _____

How many students at the school? _____

How many students in the class? _____

How many teachers? _____

How many teacher aides? _____

Age range of students? _____

What do the behavioral needs look like? Is there a visible management plan in place? Describe: _____

_____

_____

Functional and academic level of class: _____

_____

Types of disabilities served in the class: _____

_____

_____

Describe what the classroom looks like (including what is on the walls, how desks or tables are set up, etc.): _____

_____

_____

_____

_____

What's the overall atmosphere of the classroom? (noise, mood, etc.): __

_____

_____

_____

Do students interact with each other? _____

_____

_____

_____

_____

Do students go to specials? (music, art, gym): _____

_____

Do students go to the lunchroom? _____

_____

Do students go to recess? _____

_____

What is the schedule of a typical day? _____

_____

_____

_____

Teacher credentials and special certifications: _____

_____

Curriculum/philosophy of teaching?_____

_____

_____

_____

Visible modifications and accommodations: _____

_____

_____

_____

Behavioral interventions used: _____

_____

_____

_____

How do related services work? (e.g., counseling, speech, OT, PT) _____

_____

_____

_____

Other observations: _____

_____

_____

_____

_____

_____

Sample Form: Parent Communication/Phone Log

Keep the communication log in your records binder and make note of every conversation, phone call, and e-mail you have with the school or providers regarding your child.

▼ **PARENT COMMUNICATION LOG**

Date and Form of Contact	With Whom?	Initiated by:	Reason:	Discussion/ Outcome:

Date and Form of Contact	With Whom?	Initiated by:	Reason:	Discussion/ Outcome:

Sample Form: Concerns about School-Related Issues Chart

Keeping track of what is worrying you about how your child is doing in school can help make your point when you talk to the teacher. Write down your concerns and observations and fill in the report cards, notes home, homework, and other paperwork that support your concerns. Make note, too, of anything that has been tried at school or at home to help your child.

▼ CONCERNS ABOUT SCHOOL-RELATED ISSUES

Concerns	Supporting Evidence Concerns	Possible Related Factors	Interventions, Accommodations Tried/Suggested	Assessments Need	Team Decisions

Concerns	Supporting Evidence Concerns	Possible Related Factors	Interventions, Accommodations Tried/Suggested	Assessments Need	Team Decisions

Sample Form: Antecedent, Behavior, Consequence Chart (ABC Chart)

An ABC chart looks at the **a**ntecedent, (the circumstances or triggering situation that occurs right before the behavior), the **b**ehavior, (what your child does or how she reacts), and the **c**onsequences, (what happens as a result of the behavior).

Where did this occur?	Antecedent (What happened before the behavior occurred?)	Behavior (Describe what your child did, how he reacted, etc.)	Consequence (Describe what happened as a result of the behavior)

Where did this occur?	Antecedent (What happened before the behavior occurred?)	Behavior (Describe what your child did, how he reacted, etc.)	Consequence (Describe what happened as a result of the behavior)

Sample Form: Records Binder Checklist

Keep this checklist in the front of your three-ring records binder to make sure you have your child's important records and paperwork gathered in one place.

- ○ Concerns about School-Related Issues chart. You may want to keep blank copies in your binder, too.
- ○ School handbook and/or policy information and a school calendar
- ○ Medical information, including recent reports related to your child's disability as well as names and contact information for medical personnel
- ○ Contact information of services providers, evaluators, and school personnel
- ○ Reports cards, progress reports, and standardized test results
- ○ Awards and achievements your child has received. If you don't have certificates, make a list.
- ○ Communication logs and printed e-mails.
- ○ Letters and notes to and from the school and service providers.
- ○ Copy of the completed Referral for Evaluation and Consent to Evaluate forms
- ○ Copy of your *Parental Rights and Procedural Safeguards* (the parents' rights and responsibilities booklet)

○ Prior written notice(s) for meetings.

○ Evaluation reports

○ Meeting notes and notices

○ 504 plans and accompanying documentation

○ Individualized educational program (IEP) and associated documentation, including a behavior intervention plan (if your child has one)

○ Notices regarding disciplinary action and/or suspension notices

○ Samples of schoolwork, especially those that show improvement or
struggle on your child's part.

○ Blank notebook paper for taking notes

○ Other _____

Sample Form: Parent Addendum to IEP Page

Your child's school may use an IEP that has an addendum page available. If
not, you may add one on a piece of paper or bring a copy of this form with
you just in case you need it. Make sure to note on the signature page that
you have disagreements that are noted on the attached addendum page.

Attachment A: Parent Addendum Page of: your full name(s)

IEP for: your child's full name

Date:

We have the following concerns about the IEP recommendations, document, discussion, or evaluations considered at this meeting:

_____

_____

_____

_____

_____

_____

_____

_____

_____

_____

APPENDIX D

Support and Advocacy Resources

General Resources on Disabilities, Disability Rights, and Special Education

CONSORTIUM FOR APPROPRIATE DISPUTE RESOLUTION IN SPECIAL EDUCATION (CADRE)

P.O. Box 51360
Eugene, OR 97405-0906
541-686-5060
www.directionservice.org/cadre

CADRE is the National Center on Dispute Resolution in Special Education, a project of the TA&D Network. The website has comprehensive resources on mediation and conflict resolution, plus training materials. It also has listings of conflict resolution professionals and state information about mediation.

COUNCIL FOR EXCEPTIONAL CHILDREN (CEC)

2900 Crystal Drive, Suite 1000
Arlington, VA 22202
888-232-7733
www.cec.sped.org

The CEC is a leader in special education advocacy. It works to improve public policy regarding children and youth with disabilities and gifts and talents, their parents, and the professionals who work with them, at all levels of government. In addition to providing information about policies and legislation, the CEC has a large online resource bank of information about exceptionalities, special education, assessment, evidence-based practices, and inclusion.

DISABILITY RIGHTS EDUCATION AND DEFENSE FUND (DREDF)

3075 Adeline Street, Suite 210
Berkeley, CA 94703
510-644-2555
FAX/TTY: 510-841-8645
www.dredf.org

DREDF is a civil rights law and policy center run by and dedicated to parents of children who have disabilities. The center provides legal advocacy, training, education, and information about policies and rights. DREDF aims to help parents become better advocates for their children by helping them have the tools and information needed to speak up for what their children need. They educate lawyers, service providers, government officials, and others about disability civil rights laws and policies.

SPECIAL NEEDS ALLIANCE (SNA)

6341 E. Brian Kent Drive
Tucson, AZ 85710
520-546-1005
Toll-free: 877-572-8472
Fax: 520-546-5119
www.specialneedsalliance.org

The SNA is a national, nonprofit organization of attorneys experienced in the practice of disability law. The alliance provides local referrals for families who are in need of the advice of a disability rights attorney.

**THE NATIONAL DISABILITY
RIGHTS NETWORK (NDRN)**
900 Second Street NE, Suite 211
Washington, DC 20002
202-408-9514
Fax: 202-408-9520
TTY: 220-408-9521
www.ndrn.org

The NDRN is a nonprofit organization for the federally mandated Protection and Advocacy (P&A) Systems and the Client Assistance Programs (CAP) for individuals with disabilities. It is the largest provider of legal advocacy services for people with disabilities. They provide training, technical assistance, and legal support.

**THE NATIONAL DISSEMINATION CENTER FOR
CHILDREN WITH DISABILITIES (NICHCY)**
www.nichcy.org

The National Dissemination Center for Children with Disabilities website is one of the most comprehensive sources of information about disabilities in children and youth, programs and services, IDEA, and research-based instruction and intervention practices for children with disabilities.

WRIGHTSLAW
www.wrightslaw.com

Wrightslaw is leading website about special education law and advocacy. Run by attorneys and special education advocates Peter and Pamela Wright, the website has thousands of articles, information about ground-breaking legal cases, and free resources for accurate, up-to-date information about special education rights, law, and advocacy.

Parent Groups and Resources

**PARENT TECHNICAL ASSISTANCE CEN-
TER NETWORK PARENT CENTER LISTING**
*www.parentcenternetwork.org/parentcenter
listing.html*

Every state in the nation has at least one Parent Training and Information (PTI) Center funded by the U.S. Department of Education, Office of Special Education Programs. The centers provide information, training, and resources for parent access in order to help parents be more informed in meeting the educational and community needs of children with disabilities. The Parent Technical Assistance Center Network is the clearinghouse for finding the nearest center in your area.

PARENT TO PARENT USA
2030 M St. NW, Suite 350
Washington, DC 20036
www.p2pusa.org

As an organization, Parent to Parent (P2P) offers support for parents who have a child with disabilities or health needs. The organization matches experienced parents with new parents for emotional support and helps locate local resources and information related to your child's specific needs.

THE NATIONAL FEDERATION OF FAMILIES FOR CHILDREN'S MENTAL HEALTH

9605 Medical Center Drive, Suite 280
Rockville, MD 20850
240-403-1901
Fax: 240-403-1909
www.ffcmh.org

The National Federation of Families for Children's Mental Health is a national organization that consists of more than 120 chapters and state organizations devoted to providing advocacy and assistance to families who have children with emotional, behavioral, or mental health issues.

THE TECHNICAL ASSISTANCE AND DISSEMINATION NETWORK (TA&D NETWORK)
www.tadnet.org

The TA&D Network is made up of forty-five centers funded by the Office of Special Education Programs. The centers provide information and technical assistance to states, schools, educational professionals, and families on topics such as dispute resolution, learning disabilities, parenting children with special needs, behavior support, and transitions support.

Resources for Specific Disabilities

AMERICAN ASSOCIATION ON INTELLECTUAL AND DEVELOPMENTAL DISABILITIES (AAIDD)

501 3rd Street NW, Suite 200
Washington, DC 20001
202-387-1968
Fax: 202-387-2193
www.aaidd.org

The AAIDD is the most current and authoritative source on intellectual disabilities. The organization has information regarding diagnosis, supports, and best practices for instruction and life skills.

AMERICAN FOUNDATION FOR THE BLIND (AFB)

2 Penn Plaza, Suite 1102
New York, NY 10121
212-502-7600
Fax: 888-545-8331
www.afb.org

The AFB connects families to knowledge and support around equal opportunities for children with vision loss. They have online courses and publications, and provide advocacy services for individuals with vision loss.

AMERICAN SPEECH-LANGUAGE-HEARING ASSOCIATION (ASHA)
2200 Research Boulevard
Rockville, MD 20850-3289
800-498-2071
Fax: 301-296-8580
TTY: 301-296-5650
www.asha.org

ASHA is the leading organization for professionals who deal with speech, language, hearing, and other related disorders. They maintain a comprehensive library of information about speech-language related disabilities and are a leader in advocacy efforts for special education. Parents can access information, find answers to questions, or find a professional in their local area.

BRAIN INJURY ASSOCIATION OF AMERICA (BIAA)
1608 Spring Hill Road, Suite 110
Vienna, VA 22182
703-761-0750
Fax: 703-761-0755
www.biausa.org

BIAA is a source of information for families and individuals affected by traumatic brain injuries. The organization provides information on research, treatment, and the effects of brain injuries, and can connect parents to a local chapter.

CHILDREN AND ADULTS WITH ATTENTION-DEFICIT/HYPERACTIVITY DISORDER (CHADD)
8181 Professional Place, Suite 150
Landover, MD 20785
301-306-7070

Fax: 301-306-7090
www.chadd.org

CHADD is the nation's leading nonprofit organization providing education, support, and advocacy for families and individuals with ADHD.

NATIONAL CENTER FOR LEARNING DISABILITIES (NCLD)
381 Park Avenue South, Suite 1401
New York, NY 10016
212-545-7510
Fax: 212-545-9665
Toll-free: 888-575-7373
www.ncld.org

NCLD offers a tremendous amount of information, toolkits, suggestions, and planning tools for parents of children who have learning and attention issues and ADHD.

NATIONAL CONSORTIUM ON DEAF-BLINDNESS (NCDB)
800-438-9376
Fax: 503-838-8150
TTY: 800-854-7013
www.nationaldb.org

NCDB is a national assistance and dissemination center for children and youth who are deaf-blind. Funded by the U.S. Department of Education's Office of Special Education Programs, NCDB's website can help connect parents with a deaf-blindness project in their state.

NATIONAL DOWN SYNDROME CONGRESS (NDSC)
30 Mansell Court, Suite 108
Roswell, GA 30076
800-232-NDSC (6372)
www.ndsccenter.org

NDSC is a leading source of information on Down syndrome, providing a number of different resources and materials in different formats to help parents have the support they need to raise a child with Down syndrome.

OASIS @ MAAP
P.O. Box 524
Crown Point, IN 46308
219-662-1311
www.aspergersyndrome.org

The Online Asperger Syndrome Information and Support (OASIS), now joined with MAAP Services for Autism and Asperger Syndrome, is a resource for information, networking, and referrals for families and individuals affected by autism spectrum disorders.

Resources for Early Intervention

CENTER ON THE SOCIAL AND EMOTIONAL FOUNDATIONS FOR EARLY LEARNING (CSEFEL)
Dept. of Special Ed, Box 328 GPC, Vanderbilt University
Nashville, TN 37203
615-322-8150
http://csefel.vanderbilt.edu

CSEFEL is devoted to promoting social-emotional development and school readiness skills in children from birth to age five. It's a national resource center for training and technical assistance that provides materials and information about research-based practices for helping social-emotional development and preventing and managing challenging behaviors.

THE EARLY CHILDHOOD TECHNICAL ASSISTANCE CENTER (ECTA)
CB 8040
Chapel Hill, NC 27599-8040
919-962-2001
Fax: 919-966-7463
www.ectacenter.org

ECTA is funded by the Office of Special Education Programs and is in place to improve state early intervention and early childhood special education service systems. The website has a number of resources for parents including general information about early intervention and very specific information about parental rights.

Resources for Transition Planning

CENTER ON EDUCATION AND WORK (CEW)
1025 West Johnson Street, Room #964
Madison, WI 53706-1796
800-862-1071
www.cew.wisc.edu

CEW provides workshops, training, and technical assistance for children who will be transitioning from special education services to the community. The goal is to improve the connection between education and work for individuals with disabilities and learning needs.

HEATH RESOURCE CENTER
The George Washington University
2134 G Street NW
Washington, DC 20052
www.heath.gwu.edu

The HEATH Resource Center at the National Youth Transitions Center is a comprehensive online information clearinghouse about postsecondary educational opportunities for students with disabilities. The HEATH Center has information on all different types of schools and provides toolkits and training modules around all the areas of college life.

Index